Introduction

"The illiterate of the twenty-first century will not be those who cannot read and write, but those who cannot learn, unlearn and relearn."

Alvin Toffler, Author of Future Shock and *Think Like Einstein*

We are genetically encoded to learn and children are natural learners. For them the process of learning is a journey of exploration and discovery. Learning therefore should be fun.

Today we know more about how children learn than ever before. Then why is it that so many adults have a negative attitude towards maths?

As a headteacher I was unhappy with the way maths was introduced to young children. They were often rushed into the closed world of work sheets and 'sums' before they had a grasp of basic mathematical concepts. They lacked understanding and were forced to resort to blindly follow a set of prescribed rules. A whole world of pattern and relationships had been closed to them.

Book 1 & 2 of Child's Play Maths is a program that introduces maths concepts to children through the natural process of play, games and open ended activities. Adopting this approach through the medium of Cuisenaire rods, the most precise arithmetical model ever devised, ensures young children gain an understanding of maths concepts generally considered too advanced for them.

The rods themselves embrace all the learning styles and provide links to language and art. They help children access the most powerful abilities the brain possesses and this 'brain friendly' approach is often referred to as 'whole brain' or 'accelerated' learning.

This program is not just about maths – it is about learning, specifically learning how to learn. Through interaction with the program your child will acquire generic learning skills that will stand him/her in good stead whatever activity he/she is engaged in.

If you are considering using this program at home then be assured it does not matter what particular scheme your child may be following in school. It is not 'the rods' that are being taught but math concepts through the rods that lead to a deep understanding of the true nature of the underlying pattern and relationships that form the rich world of mathematics.

At the end of the book you will find a link to our innovative software app that simulates the rods. Currently it only works with Windows but a Mac version is in the process of being developed.

"I love this approach to teaching math with my students. . ."Eugenia B. (Teacher)

"This is a wonderful program. . . I highly recommend this product and this ingenious approach to Math."
Christine Hindle – The Old Schoolhouse Magazine.

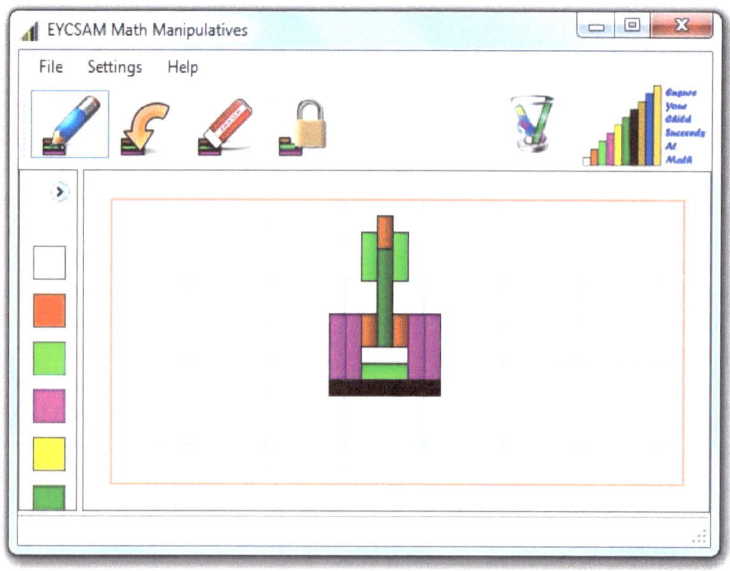

We sincerely believe this program reflects the findings of Alison Gobnik, Ph.D., Andrew N. Meltzoff, Ph.D., Patricia K.Kuhl, Ph. D.

"Walk upstairs, open the door gently, and look in the crib. What do you see? Most of us see a picture of innocence and helplessness, a clean slate. But, in fact, what we see in the crib is the greatest mind that has ever existed, the most powerful learning machine in the universe."

From *"The Scientist in the Crib"*

If you have any questions or need help at any time please email me at: **phil@helpyourchildsucceed.com** and I will get back to you ASAP

Child's Play Maths 1 & 2

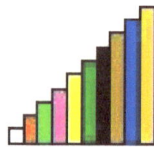

UNIT 1   About Cuisenaire Rods

UNIT 2   Cuisenaire Rods & the School Curriculum

UNIT 3   Incidental Learning

UNIT 4   Vocabulary

UNIT 5   Important Words and Phrases

UNIT 6   Developing Memory Recall

UNIT 7   Mental Imaging Games

UNIT 8   Cardinal Number

UNIT 9   Staircases

UNIT 10   Staircases and Mental Agility

UNIT 11   Extended Staircases

UNIT 12   Staircases and Multiplication

UNIT 13   Language Development

UNIT 14   Introducing Signs +

UNIT 15   Signs < >

UNIT 16   Signs =

UNIT 17   Brackets

UNIT 18   Signs -

UNIT 19   Signs x

UNIT 20   Signs ÷

UNIT 21   Signs: Fractions as Operators

UNIT 22   Reviewing Where We've Been

UNIT 23   The Importance of Questions

UNIT 24   Partitions of Length

UNIT 25   Families of Equivalent Factors and Products

UNIT 26   Families of Equivalent Subtraction

UNIT 27   Families of Equivalent Fractions

UNIT 28   The First Phase: An Overview

UNIT 29   Getting Organised and Moving On

UNIT 30	Beyond the Rods
UNIT 31	Studying Families
UNIT 32	Families of Partitions (Length)
UNIT 33	Partitioning Without the Rods
UNIT 34	Time Out for Talk
UNIT 35	The Commutative Property of Addition
UNIT 36	Consolidating: Mental Substitution
UNIT 37	The 'Grain of Rice' Principle.
UNIT 38	Free Expression
UNIT 39	Families of Equivalent Difference
UNIT 40	Extending the Challenge
UNIT 41	Families of Factors and Divisors
UNIT 42	Factor Families: The Commutative Property
UNIT 43	Factor Families: Consolidation
UNIT 44	Factor Families
UNIT 45	Numbers Have Names

UNIT 46	Families of Equivalent Fractions and Quotients
UNIT 47	Equivalent Fraction Families: Generating Staircases
UNIT 48	Reciprocal Fractions
UNIT 49	The Importance of Review
UNIT 50	Looking Forward
UNIT 51	Families of Equivalent Difference
UNIT 52	Families of Equivalent fractions: >
UNIT 53	Families of Equivalent Fractions: <
UNIT 54	Families of Equivalent Fractions: Adam and Eve
UNIT 55	Families of Equivalent Fractions: Reproduction
UNIT 56	Families of Equivalent Addition
UNIT 57	Families of Equivalent Products
UNIT 58	Families of Equivalent Fractions
UNIT 59	Accelerated Learning

UNIT 60   Points Worth Remembering

UNIT 61   Introducing Number Names: Part 1

UNIT 62   Introducing Number Names: Part 2

UNIT 63   Introducing Number Names: Part 3

UNIT 64   Journey's End?

Child's Play Maths

Books 1 & 2

Ages 3 - 11

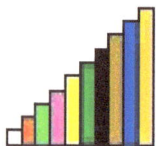

UNIT 1: About Cuisenaire Rods

WHY CUISENAIRE RODS?
They are simply the best tool available for introducing and teaching maths to children (and adults) of all ages.

Developments within **brain-based research** confirm the rods as having many of the essential attributes to ensure children learn as effectively as they can.

They are particularly effective for all types of learners – **visual**, **auditory** and **kinaesthetic** (hands-on).

CUISENAIRE RODS
The rods are simply cuboids of coloured wood or plastic.
The smallest, white, is a 1 cm cube. The longest, orange, is a 10 cm long cuboid.
Just like a piano – once the basics have been mastered the rods hold within themselves infinite mathematical possibilities.

Children of all ages benefit from using the rods.
They stimulate insight and understanding from the basic concept of equivalence to Pythagoras' Theorem.

Colour - a greater stimulus to memory recall than verbal cues or objects.

Imagination – Albert Einstein imagined himself travelling on a sunbeam and the theory of relativity was born.

Imaging - 90% of all information that comes to our brain is visual.

This approach can be followed alongside any scheme of work and **is the perfect program for introducing maths to children at home or school.**

Manual Dexterity – Constant manipulation of the fingers has a positive impact on the mind.

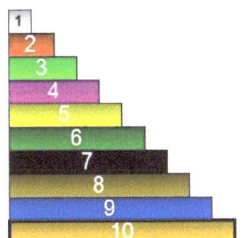

The Big Picture - Children need the global overview the rods provide naturally.

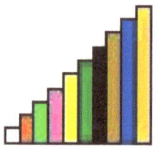

UNIT 2: Cuisenaire and the School Curriculum

HOW DOES THIS FIT IN WITH THE SCHOOL CURRICULUM?

The program teaches universal maths concepts in a way that is totally child-centred.

Children discover maths is creative and fun. Concepts are discovered through play, games and open-ended challenges.

The program is designed to compliment the way children learn best and because of this children's learning is invariably accelerated compared to children exposed to more traditional and formal methods.

Maths need no longer be the source of stress and conflict.

HOW DO I START?
Just give the rods to a child of any age and he/she will do what they do best – play.

Play creates a positive learning environment.

Directed activities can be introduced alongside free play to reflect children's particular interests. There are no limits to the possibilities

Play is one of the most powerful motivational forces in the world. Learning should always be fun – structured, but fun.

Most of our learning is non-conscious and incidental.

Play is the harvesting of experience that will feed the growth of the child's understanding and further development.

Create your own star ship. Play stimulates that most important attribute of the brain – **imagination**.

UNIT 3: Incidental Learning

INCIDENTAL OR NON-CONSCIOUS LEARNING

Most of our learning is non-conscious. Schools make use of displays to communicate information to children.

This kind of 'information immersion' is used to good effect by advertisers.
Just think how easily children 'learn' a tune or pop-song.

Whilst 'playing' with the rods children will have made many important discoveries (see opposite).

In this way children will begin to acquire their number bonds without even realising it.

e g 10 = 4 + 6 = 2 + 8 = 7 + 3 = 9 + 1

1. Rods of the same colour are also equal in length.

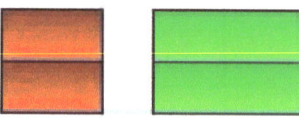

2. Rods of the same length are equal in colour.

3. Rods of different colours have different lengths.

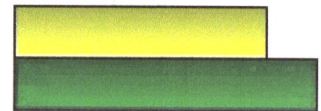

4. It is possible to make equal lengths by putting rods end to end.

At a later stage, when they are asked what two numbers make ten, children will be able to visualise the pattern for ten.

Fingers will definitely not be needed!

5. Observe children and you may see them beginning to organise their work. The pattern below reveals an understanding of the commutative property of addition.

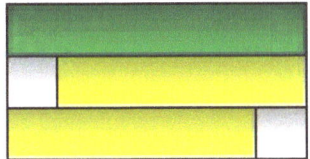

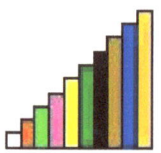

UNIT 4: Vocabulary

VOCABULARY – ALGEBRA BEFORE ARITHMETIC

The program introduces children to **algebra before arithmetic.** This is because number is an abstract concept and difficult for young children to grasp.

It is easier for children to learn basic maths concepts via algebra before being Introduced to number.

When number is eventually introduced for addition, subtraction, multiplication and division, children have no problem because the concepts are already familiar to them.

Young children can be introduced to the vocabulary over a period of time. Older children will grasp it very quickly.

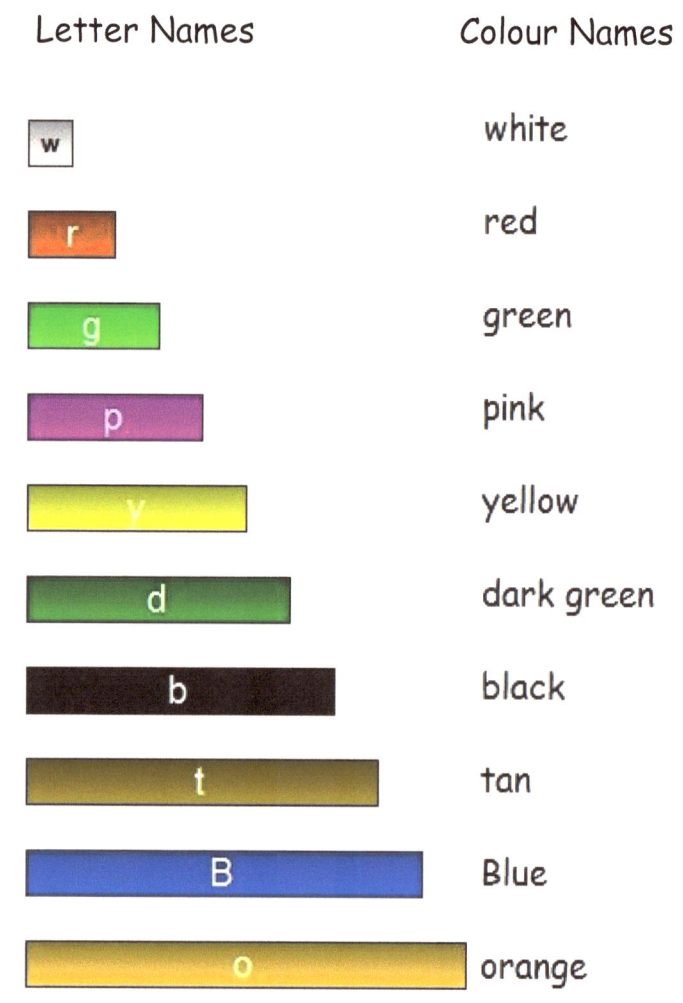

Letter Names	Colour Names
w	white
r	red
g	green
p	pink
y	yellow
d	dark green
b	black
t	tan
B	Blue
o	orange

Young children are quick to understand that : 'o' represents orange.

They will eventually write 'sentences' or equations they have made and can visualise in their head.
e.g. t + r = o

Later they will have no problem exchanging 'number names' for 'letter names'.
e g 8 + 2 = 10

Visualising or mental imaging is just one of the abilities the brain possesses and needs to be encouraged and developed.

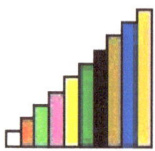# UNIT 5: Vocabulary (Cont'd)

IMPORTANT WORDS AND PHRASES:

All children need to know this vocabulary. For young children it can be introduced during **FREE PLAY** or **DIRECTED ACTIVITIES**.

Because young children are more naturally kinaesthetic learners introducing the vocabulary this way will ensure they understand and retain it.

This is also true for older children or adults who, for whatever reason, did not understand these concepts the first time around.

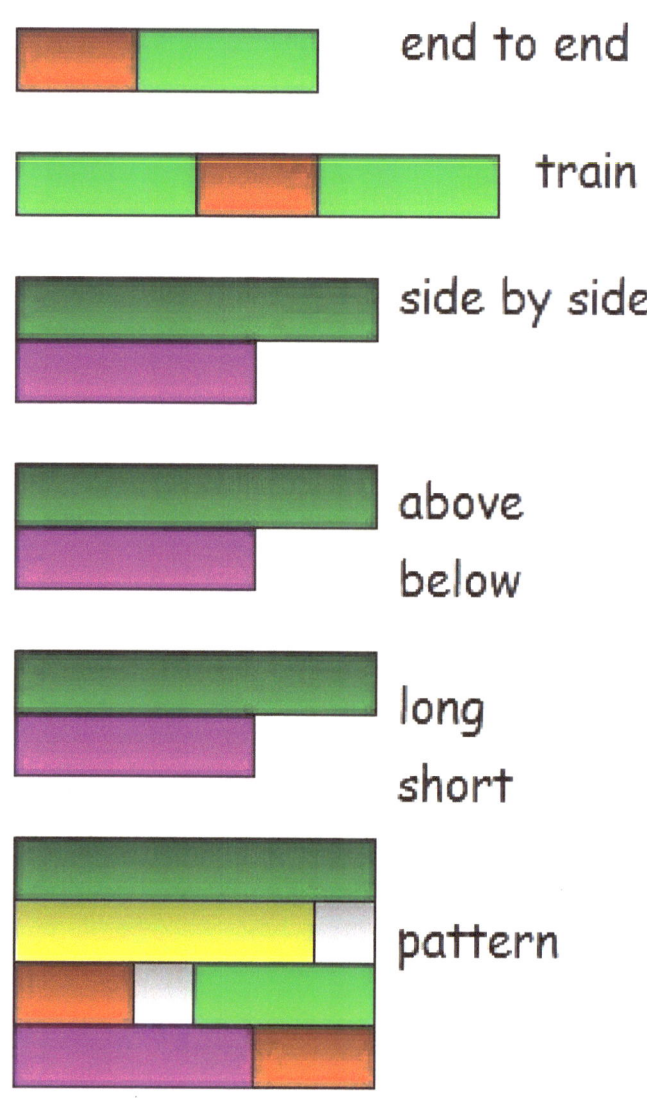

Adults have found this approach very liberating especially as, often for the first time, they are able to 'see' patterns and relationships that traditional teaching methods had 'hidden' from them.

I hear and I forget,
I see and I remember
I do and I understand,
Chinese Proverb

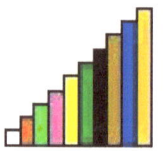 # UNIT 6: Developing Memory Recall

LEARNING EQUATION:
L = U + M
Learning equals understanding plus memory.
This programme is built upon the foundation of understanding and not learning by rote.

The kinaesthetic approach afforded by the rods provides the understanding. This must be consolidated by memory recall. We remember via our senses. You can begin to increase children's capacity for recall now by engaging his/her senses in every activity.

We have all experienced an occasion when a smell, a sound, a colour, or a particular taste triggers memories we often did not know we possessed.

Imagination and the Senses

If your children want to build a fairy tale castle with the rods then ask them to imagine themselves standing outside the castle first.

What might they see, smell, hear, taste? Get them to 'see' the object they are about to create in their mind.

The smell of leather transports me back to my first day in school. I see murals on the wall that have long since disappeared. Experience once again the panic of being abandoned by my mother for a whole day!

Colour, for example, is a greater stimulus for memory recall than verbal cues or objects. (Backman et al and Allen)

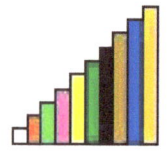

UNIT 7: Mental Imaging Games

GAMES TO DEVELOP MENTAL IMAGING – VISUALISATION

"I never think in words, only pictures."
Thomas Alva Edison

The ability for children to possess a mental image of the rods is vital as this will speed up progress considerably.

FREE PLAY should continue alongside activities where you offer more direction.
e g *"Build Cinderella's castle using only red and white rods."*

Apparently Albert Einstein first became interested in the Theory of Relativity after imagining himself travelling on a beam of light. Daydreaming, exercising our imagination, is one of the brain's most powerful abilities.

Ask children to hold their hands behind their back. Give them two rods to hold. Can they guess which colours?

As they become more confident increase the level of difficulty by giving them three or four rods at a time.

Try placing rods in a bag as children becomes more skilled at guessing.

If the game becomes too easy children will get bored. Too difficult and they will be discouraged. You are the person best equipped to pitch it just right for your children and provide them with the optimum state for learning.

Another of the senses, touch, is now introduced via games – 'touch games'.

These games are designed to ensure children can recognise the rods by touch alone.

Although colour is a powerful stimulus for memory recall and understanding it is possible for children with impaired vision or no vision at all to derive tremendous benefit from the rods.

Children who have little or no sight usually develop this sensory ability to a very high degree. It has been suggested that rather than being disabled these children should be regarded as differently-abled. (Eric Jenson)

Noted psychologist Mihaly Csikzentmihalyi has described **the 'flow state'** as being the required state of consciousness to ensure optimal learning takes place. It is possible to get into this 'flow' state by following a simple formula:

"(When) challenges are greater than your skill, that's anxiety. When your skills exceed the challenge that's boredom." You know when your children are bored or anxious and you are the best person to adjust the task to match the skill. You can ensure children are in the flow state every day.

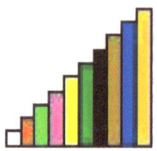

UNIT 8: Cardinal Number

CARDINAL NUMBER: "No more fingers!"

Formal approaches to the teaching of number tend to focus on one to one relationships.

This can often result in children having to count on fingers to calculate the answer to a problem. They are unable to 'see' numbers as a whole group.

Through FREE PLAY, DIRECTED ACTIVITIES and TOUCH GAMES children naturally view numbers as complete groupings.

They will know that green is equivalent to three whites while perceiving it to be a 'number' in its own right.

The concept of cardinal number has been naturally acquired through play.

Children view green (3) and red (2) as complete objects (groups) that combine to make another complete object (group), yellow (5):

g + r = y
3 + 2 = 5

and not as separate objects combined:
(w + w + w) + (w + w) = 5w
(1 + 1 + 1) + (1 + 1) = 5 (Don't worry – we will deal with brackets later)

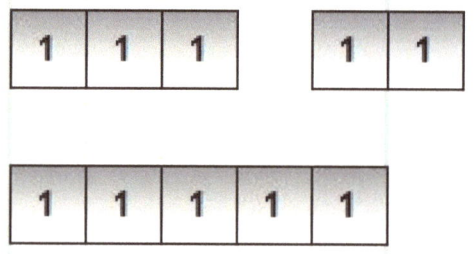

Having a firm grasp of CARDINAL NUMBER helps children develop the ability to SUBSTITUTE ONE TERM FOR ANOTHER – crucial to understanding in Maths.

NUMBER BOND GAMES can consolidate this ability and give children a firm grasp of number bonds even before 'number names' are introduced.

 Choose one of the rods and ask children to name two rods that end to end will be the same length as it.

UNIT 9: Staircases

STAIRCASES

Staircases are very potent mathematical constructions.

Staircases:
<u>help</u> fix the mental image of the rods in your child's mind;
<u>improve</u> memory recall;
<u>prepare</u> for the introduction of number and place value;
can <u>introduce</u> the early concept of fractions.

Quite probably children will have already begun to construct staircases with the rods during FREE PLAY.

Call the rods by their colour names. Later, when all the signs have been introduced, children will write sentences using the letter-names of the rods.

Children will quite possibly have already made a staircase like the one below.

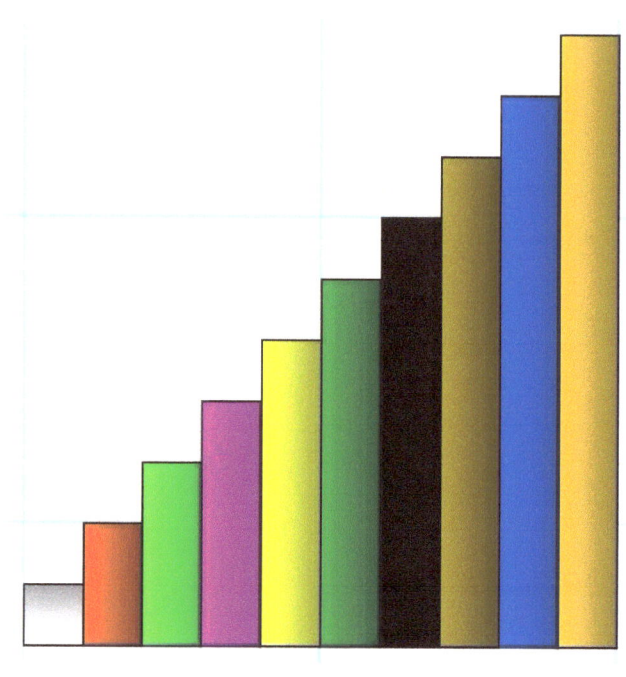

The sequence is:

w, r, g, p, y, d, b, t, B, o

1, 2, 3, 4, 5, 6, 7, 8, 9, 10

Explain that because the colour names begin with a certain initial letter they will be given that letter name.

We call brown 'tan' because we already have a black (b) and a blue (B).

Because blue is bigger we write the initial letter in upper case.

Tan becomes 't'.

There is an important link to language development here that we will look at later.

If children have not made any staircases ask them to make a set of stairs starting with the smallest rod (white) and finishing with the largest (orange).

Once we have introduced the 'number names' of the rods the white will, most of the time but not always, represent 1.

It is vital that the rods are not seen to represent a particular number.

For example when introducing fractions we may decide to call red 'one'. We will look at this next

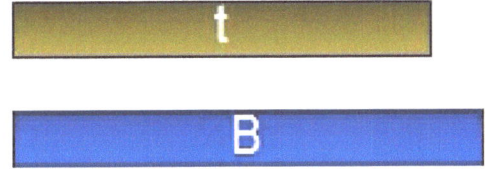

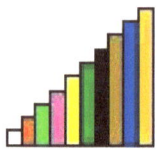

UNIT 10: Mental Agility

MENTAL AGILITY

Mental Agility - It is important that children never associate a rod with a particular number. The rods are not a cumbersome calculating tool.

They represent a complete arithmetical model designed to free them to think in abstract terms.

This is important for later work, for example, with fractions and graphs.

One way of doing this is getting children to visualise a staircase and name the rods going up and going down.

In this way, depending on whether the child has built the complete staircase or not, red will be viewed as 'step 2' going up and 'step 4' going down.

Make staircases using the first five colours and ask children to visualise and then 'read them going up and going down.'

Increase the challenge as children get more adept. e g the first six, seven rods etc. Remember the 'flow state'.

RELATIONSHIP GAMES
Play these games regularly once children have been introduced to the 'number names' of the rods:

"If red has the value of one which rod is two, three, etc.?"

Later, once children are introduced to the 'number names' of the rods, play RELATIONSHIP GAMES to help increase your child's mental agility.

The early concept of FRACTIONS – the idea that numbers exist between 'whole numbers' - can be introduced using this approach.

Because children have experienced pleasure in using the rods creatively during FREE PLAY they will always adopt a positive attitude to the introduction of new concepts. The material is familiar and associated with positive experiences.

Learning is fun!

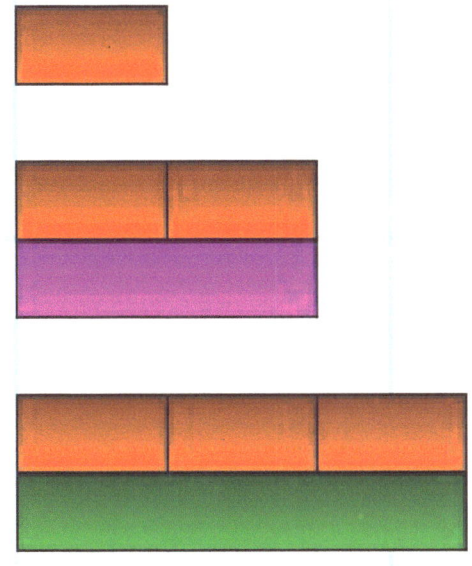

Choose different rods to represent one.

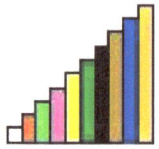

UNIT 11: Extended Staircases

EXTENDED STAIRCASES

Staircases can be extended beyond the first ten steps just as numbers can extend beyond ten to infinity.

Ask children to continue their staircase beyond the orange rod,

Some can 'see' the next step immediately. Others will resort to trial and error – very scientific.
Some will be baffled – not a good learning state!

While it is important to present a challenge once a situation becomes stressful learning will not take place. Mental blocks are often the result of imposed stressful learning situations.

Many of us believe we are 'no good' at maths because we were frequently exposed to formal maths situations before we were ready.

CINDERELLA'S STAIRCASE

Cinderella wants a staircase with white carpet.
Can you build it?

Once they reach orange suggest they have more carpet left.
Can they continue up the staircase?

The Cockroft Report found many professional people, including teachers, felt guilty about their lack of expertise in maths.

Instead why not exercise the imagination. A very powerful learning ally. We shall call this game: CINDERELLA'S STAIRCASE

These games and challenges are a preparation for the understanding of different number bases.

Later children will be led to see how our number system is constructed and also how it is possible to work in bases other than ten

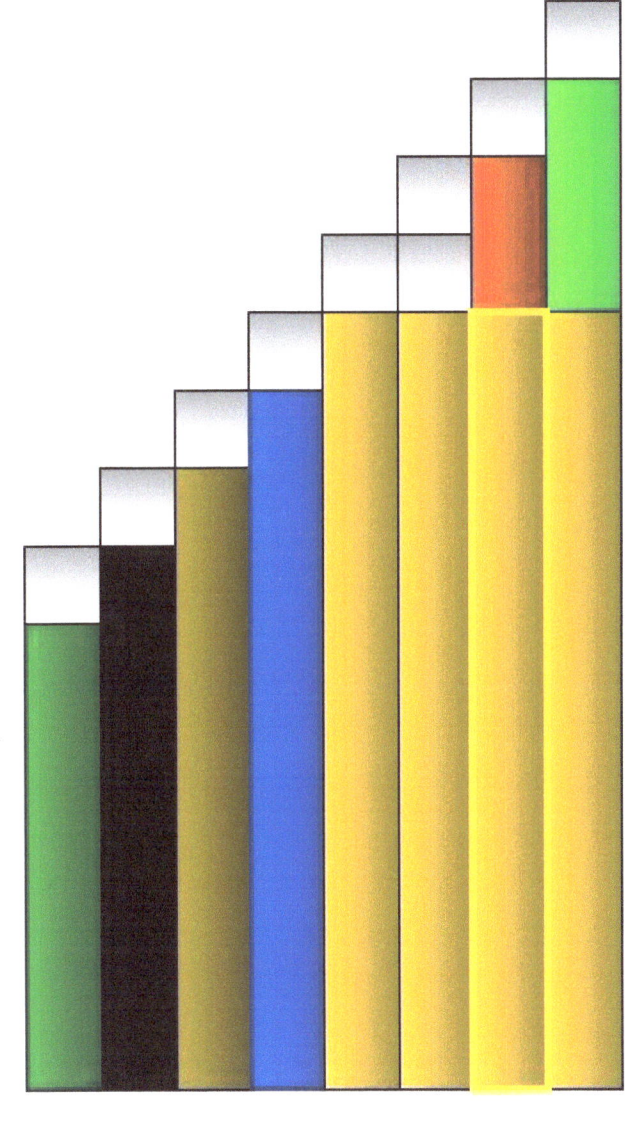

UNIT 12: Staircases

PREPARATION FOR MULTIPLICATION

Colour plays an important role in learning. It aids memory recall and understanding.

Maths is a rich landscape of pattern and relationship. The rods open a window through which this vibrant world is visible to children.

Multiplication is simply repeated addition (iteration). It is closely related to division and factors of numbers.

Each multiplication table has a distinct pattern that can be revealed by the rods. By adding a 'twist' to Cinderella's Staircase children can be introduced to multiplication tables.

Simply suggest that Cinderella wishes to change her carpet to red. What would the staircase look like now?

Cinderella's Red Carpet.
(The two times table).
If necessary construct the first two or three steps and ask children to continue.

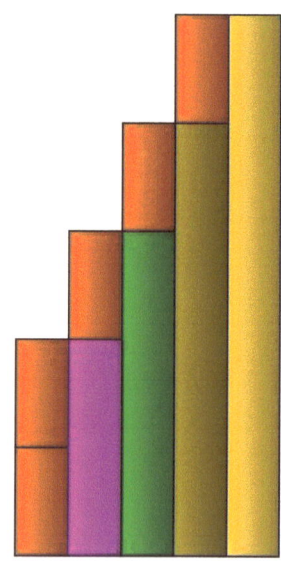

The sequence is:
r, p, d, t, o...
2, 4, 6, 8, 10,...
1 x 2, 2 x 2, 3 x 2, 4 x 2, 5 x 2...
The difference will always be red (2)

Explain to children that *the first step of the staircase will always be the colour of the carpet.*

It is always interesting to observe how some children continue the staircase beyond the orange rod. Some will intuitively use the rods that represent multiples of the first step.

The green (3) staircase can be constructed using only green, dark green and blue:
g,   3,
d,   6,
B,   9,
(B+g) 12,
(B+d) 15 etc.

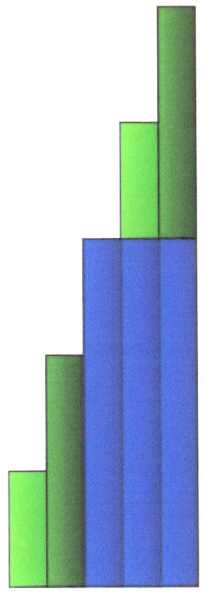

Cinderella's Green Carpet.
(The three times table).
Again construct the first two or three steps if necessary.

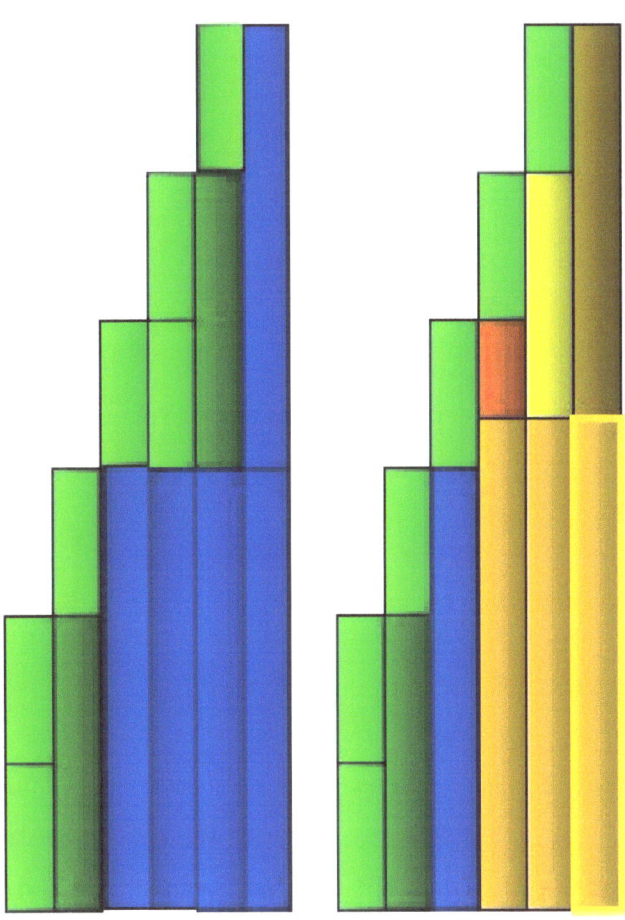

The sequence is:
g, d, B, (B+g), (B+d), (B+B)   or
g, d, B (o+r), (o+y), (o+t)
3, 6, 9, 12, 15, 18, . . .
1 x 3, 2 x 3, 3 x 3, 4 x 3, 5 x 3, 6 x 3, . . .

The difference will always be green (3)
This work also lays the foundation for understanding number bases.

UNIT 13: Language Development

HOW CAN A MATHS PROGRAMME HELP CHILDREN'S LANGUAGE DEVELOPMENT?

Well, what is language?

Most of us would agree that the primary function of language is to communicate ideas – the power to translate thought into words.

At some point we want to express those ideas in written form. Having been given plenty of opportunity to express themselves creatively with the rods children now possess a wealth of ideas that can be expressed in written form.

They have been introduced to TRAINS and have learnt how to read them from left to right. It is now only a short step to putting their thoughts into words.

Children need plenty of oral practice before they are ready to write.

They already know the letter names of the rods.

Children with dyslexic tendencies love this approach because when they eventually write 'sentences' they don't have to worry about phonics. When children start to write please don't worry about neatness. Once the SIGNS have been introduced they have everything they need to write complex mathematical sentences.

e.g. $3g + r = 2y + w$

$(3 \times 3) + 2 = (2 \times 5) + 1$

$9 + 2 = 10 + 1$

$11 = 11$

They can read the pattern as a sentence and visualise the sentence as a pattern.

The next question is HOW?

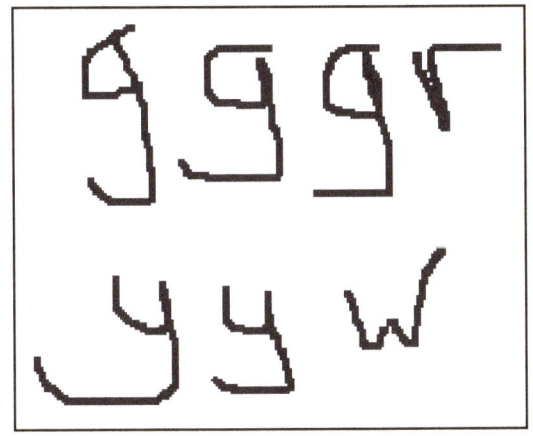

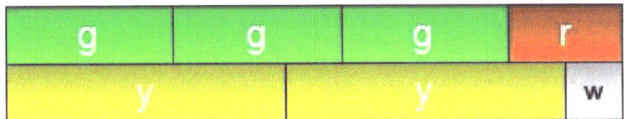

When children start to write please don't worry about neatness.

They should write big on plain paper. Let them write what they want to express about the rods.

Treat their first expressions at writing as you did their first work of art.

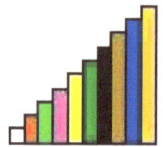

UNIT 14: Introducing Signs

THE BRAIN AND DATA

The brain enjoys detecting pattern, so the more data we give it the better.

When you introduce the signs to children do so over a short period of time.

Children will use the signs creatively just as they first used the rods. The signs will be used to construct sentences that become more complex as each new sign is introduced.

Interestingly children who are perceived to be of 'low intelligence' are often fed a limited amount of information not to confuse them. This approach ensures that is exactly what we end up doing.

With just two signs children will find ways to be creative.

With just two colours children will make a variety of TRAINS.

Write the 'letter-names' for the rods on a piece of plain paper or white board. Children can 'see' where the symbols come from.

They will now realise their constructions (trains) can be 'made' on paper.

Instead of the physical properties of the rods, colour and length, symbols now represent the distinctive differences.

The letter 'r' will evoke a mental image of the red rod.

Children have now written something which has obvious meaning to them. This is the essence of language to give spoken or written expression to our thoughts

Even if you further restrict them to just two colours they will still find ways to be creative.

How?

Well, let's start with what they already know:

1. They know the colour names of the rods.
2. They know the letter names of the rods.

What next?

r + g + r

Instead of using the term END TO END explain to children that in future you will use the expression 'plus'.

Simply show them the symbol for 'plus' +.

UNIT 15: Signs < >

EVERYDAY EXAMPLES

Which is the longest rod?

We say: "Yellow is longer/'greater than' green."
The sign is < and we can write y < g.

We can say the man is taller than the boy with confidence.

If they switch positions can we say the boy is taller than the man?

We say: "Green is smaller/'lesser than' yellow." This time we simply turn the sign around and write g < y.

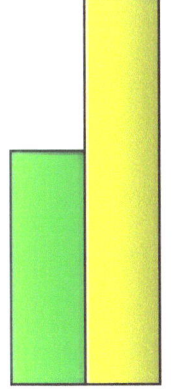

No, instead we say the boy is shorter than the man.

We will use a similar approach with the rods to introduce the sign:

'less than'   <   'greater than'.

UNIT 16: Signs =

EQUIVALENCE

The concept of equivalence is foundational to maths.

Again, everything we do must spring from children's own constructions.

This is why FREE PLAY is so vitally important. Children not only get the opportunity for an abundance of incidental learning they are forming a very positive attitude towards the rods. Working with them is creative and fun.

That is the attitude they will carry forward throughout every stage of mathematical development with the rods.

Incidentally, they are learning the correct left to right orientation for reading.

Ask children to make two trains with the rods and place them side by side.

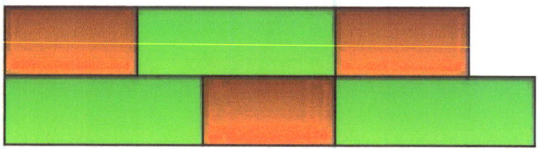

$(r + g + r) < (g + r + g)$

What must be done to make the trains equal in length (to reach a position of equivalence)? There are lots of possible solutions.

Let children try and find one for themselves. Here are just two possibilities by adding to or subtracting from the two trains.

TIP:
Before 'giving' children the symbol for equivalence ask what they think it might look like.

Remind them of what the signs for 'greater' and 'lesser than' look like.
Like arrows.
How should the 'arms' of the arrow be drawn to show 'the same as' (equivalence)?

If children do not suggest that they should be drawn side by side and the same length (parallel) then you can - but first give them the opportunity to discover it for themselves.

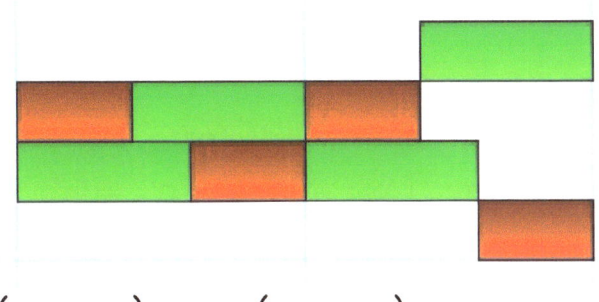

(r + g + r) + g = (g + r + g) + r

This time we remove a red rod from the first train and a green rod from the second train in order to reach a position of equivalence.

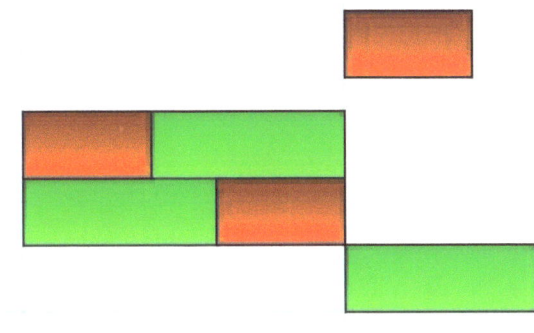

(r + g + r) - r = (g + r + g) - g

UNIT 17: Brackets

BRACKETS

Brackets or parentheses form a useful function in maths. There's no reason why children shouldn't know about them as and when they are needed. One thing they do is help sort out exactly what is going on.

For example,

d - g + r

can read:

(d - g) + r

We first undertake the action in the brackets:

(d – g) = g

We then undertake the next action.

g + r = y

It could have read:

d - (g + r)

Again we undertake the operation inside the brackets first.

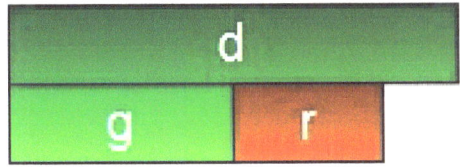

g + r = y

Then the next :

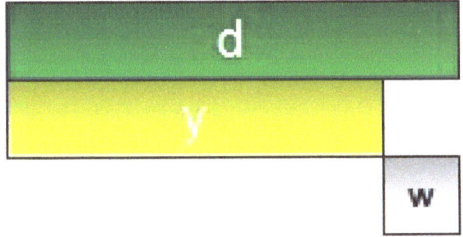

d − y = w

Use exactly the same approach with children when you introduce the **number names** of the rods.

Remember only to introduce the number names **after** children have grasped the concepts via the **letter names**.

TIP: THE ' SAY IT QUICK TECHNIQUE
You would say:
"Dark green minus green plus red." The rods you wish to group together you say quickly until children catch on. Do this lots of times with and without the rods as a game or challenge.

Children can be asked to:

1, "Hold up the rod that is equal to "yellow plus red" or "yellow minus red."

2. Increase the challenge by putting the rods away first and then asking them to shout the answer aloud.

The second challenge shows how, once familiar with the material, children can move beyond the rod and begin to abstract or work mentally.

UNIT 18: Signs -

SUBTRACTION

The introduction of the 'minus' sign is a natural progression of addition.

Begin by asking questions like:

 *"What must I add to the red rod to make it equal to the green rod?"*

Having acquired a sound mental image of the rods children should have no problems with this game.

You will probably find they can confidently play this game without the rods because they can now visualise the material.

Once it is obvious the game has been mastered you can demonstrate a quicker way of expressing it.

Play plenty of SIGN GAMES with children. They love showing off what they know. This will also aid memory retention and develop self esteem and a positive attitude.

Instead of saying "*What must I add . . .*"
Substitute this phrase with the word 'minus'.

"*Green minus red.*"

Children will now see the 'difference' between the two rods is the length of rod left uncovered by the smaller rod.

Draw the MINUS sign on paper.

Treat the introduction of every sign as a game. The more games (examples) you play the better.

TIP:
We all need to review our learning to remember it. Once you have introduced a sign play the 'game' associated with it when you introduce other signs.

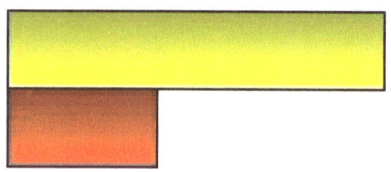

"Yellow minus red."
y - r

"Black minus green."
b - g

UNIT 19: Signs x

MULTIPLICATION

The multiplication sign can also be introduced as a natural development of addition (repeated addition). Again the game is the key.

Set children a challenge.
The challenge is to complete what is a really a simple jigsaw!

Just as we learn by our mistakes when piecing a jigsaw together why shouldn't we do the same for maths?

Children must learn to view mistakes as signposts that suggest they take a different route or small detour that will lead them closer to the objective.

"Can you make a train equal to orange using rods of only one colour?"

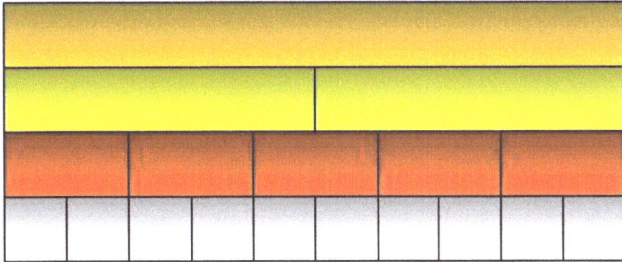

"Now read the trains using the plus and equivalence signs."

"Orange equals yellow plus yellow, equals red plus red plus red plus red plus red, equals white plus white plus white plus white plus white plus white plus white plus white plus white."

o = y + y = r + r + r + r + r = w + w + w + w + w + w + w + w + w + w

The rods are perfect for this approach.
They allow children to be challenged to the level of their own development.

That is why the formal introduction of sums before children understand the underlying concepts is so damaging.
Children become obsessed with getting it right to please teacher. If that means following a technique they learnt parrot fashion they will gladly pay the price. Real understanding must take a back seat.

Edison understood this principle perfectly. When asked how it felt to have failed a thousand times to make a light bulb work he replied:
"I have not failed a thousand times, I have found a thousand ways that did not work."

Are your children's glasses half full?

Explain it is possible to give the trains shorter and less confusing 'names'.

Instead of 'yellow plus yellow' we say two 'times' yellow or two yellows.

Do the same for the reds and whites. Write the x sign on paper. Now read: "Orange equals two times yellow, five times red, ten times white."

o = 2y = 5r = 10w

Give lots of examples

UNIT 20: Signs ÷

DIVISION

Division can be introduced in much the same way as multiplication.
We begin in exactly the same way.

Ask children to make trains of one colour equivalent to a given length.
This time start with the length represented by 'orange plus red'.

If white represents 1, then this length represents 12.
This is also a useful number to use when introducing equivalent fractions.

TIP
Later when using the number names of the rods white will usually represent 1.

It is important children do not think of white as being 1.
Any time we want we can assign white a different value which changes the value of the other rods.
For example, if white is 10 then red becomes 20.

This mental agility is important for understanding topics like graphs, fractions, area etc

Once children have completed the challenge (they needn't find them all) cover the rods and ask how many red, green, pink rods did it take to make orange plus red.

Explain that there is another way of asking the same question. We can simply say:

"Orange plus red DIVIDED by red, green, pink etc."

Draw the ÷ sign on paper.

Write (o + r) ÷ r = 6

Provide plenty of challenges. Good examples to use are tan, orange plus dark green etc.

See if children can visualise them mentally.

Read them together using the term DIVIDED.

When children are confident enough let them attempt to write the sentence.

e.g. (o + r) ÷ p = 3

Introducing the signs is a good example of how different learning styles, **VISUAL, AUDITORY, TACTILE** and **KINAESTHETIC** are blended to ensure every child is able to learn in the way that suits him/her best.

Kinaesthetic and **Tactile learners** love using the rods, **visual learners** love the colours and mental imaging while **auditory learners** enjoy the emphasis on oral work before writing.

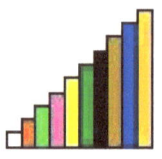 # UNIT 21: Fractions as Operators

FRACTIONS AS OPERATORS

With a little twist we can introduce the concept of fractions as operators.

Getting children to work mentally is excellent practice.

It strengthens the natural ability of imaging the brain possesses.

Begin with a review of DIVISION.

 Ask:

"How many red rods did it take to make orange and red?"
Six.

We can say that red is *six times smaller* than orange plus red.

"Which rod is three times smaller than orange plus red (pink)?"
"Which rod is two times smaller than orange plus red (dark green)?"
Repeat this for different trains.

EXPLAIN

Another way of saying 'six times smaller' is 'one sixth' written as: 1/6

1/6 x (o + r) = r   or   r = 1/6 x (o + r)

Now ask if they can find 'one fifth of orange', 'one sixth of dark green' etc.

The most difficult examples are a half, a quarter and a third because they do not sound like the number name.

TIP

Take every opportunity to review what children have learnt.

If you have introduced a new concept make sure that the following morning you review what your children learnt the day before.

Research shows that during sleep we process information we acquired the previous day.

UNIT 22: Reviewing

THE IMPORTANCE OF REVIEWING

Learning = Memory + Understanding.

Regular reviewing is vital to consolidate learning.

Children enjoy reviewing what they have learnt.

It gives them reassurance and builds self esteem.

SIGNS

We have introduced :

FREE PLAY - Children's artistic creations – talk about them.

Offer plenty of encouragement and praise.

RECORD children's work. Value it.

INCIDENTAL LEARNING
e.g. number bonds

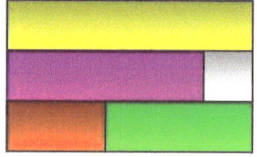

COLOUR – concepts discovered through colour before number. A powerful stimulus for memory recall.

< >

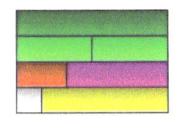

+

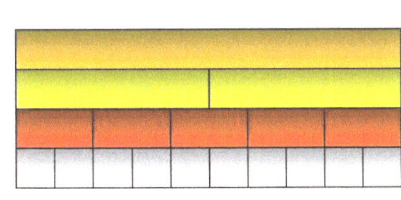

=

x

÷

¼

DIRECTED ACTIVITIES - Manipulation and improving manual dexterity stimulates the brain.

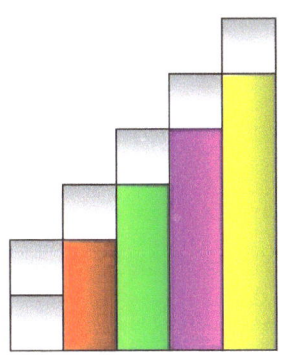

IMAGING AND VISUALISATION - Helping children acquire a retentive memory.

GAMES - To ensure children acquire a mental image of the rods.

We've even looked at brackets.
( )

These signs will enable children to 'read' what they have created in a variety of ways.

They have been introduced as games (kinaesthetic & visual); read and written as a sentence (auditory) that have become increasingly more challenging.

Our aim is for children to become fluent at 'reading' mathematical sentences (equations) .

Children need plenty of opportunity for oral work before attempting to write. Their ability to read will always be in advance of their ability to write.

What is vital is that everything is treated as a game to be enjoyed for the sheer pleasure of playing.

Encouragement and praise should be the climate.

SIGNS - Signs and the link between learning to read and write and the phonetic language of the alphabet. Introducing the signs over a short period of time.

VOCABULARY - Introducing colour names.

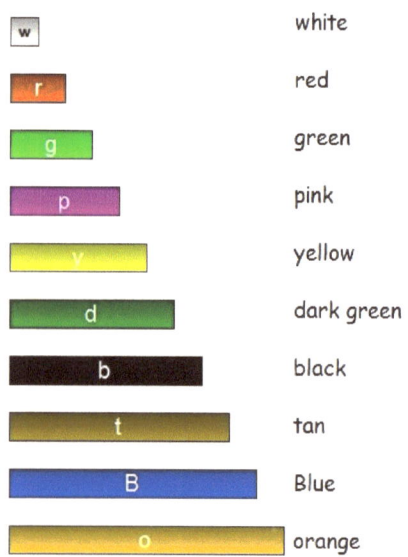

w	white
r	red
g	green
p	pink
y	yellow
d	dark green
b	black
t	tan
B	Blue
o	orange

VOCABULARY - Introducing basic vocabulary during sessions of free play and onwards. Introducing the initial letter names.

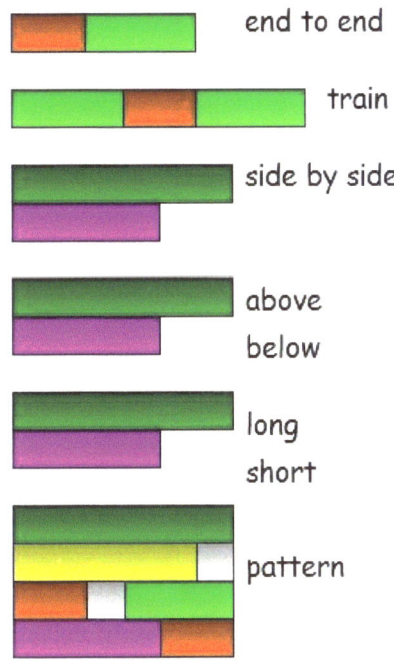

STAIRCASES - used for recall up/down.

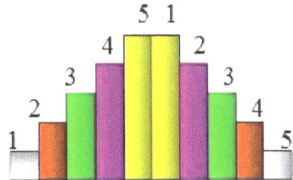

UNIT 23: Questions

THE IMPORTANCE OF QUESTIONS

Apparently Einsten's mother never asked him what he learnt at school. Instead she would ask him what questions he asked.

By over-emphasising the importance of answers we can forget that **asking the right question is by far the most creative and demanding skill.**

We now want to provide children with opportunities to study some basic maths concepts.

CLOSED AND OPEN QUESTIONS

CLOSED:

"What must I add to the red rod to make a train equal to the pink rod?"

p = r + w + w = r + r

4 = 2 + 1 + 1 = 2 + 2

Here there are only two possible answers and little opportunity for exploration and discovery of all the possibilities.

OPEN:

"How many trains can I make equal to the pink rod?"

First through creative play, then by 'reading' what has been created and finally writing it in the ideographic language of mathematics.

At each step we will use open-ended questions to pose problems children will attempt to solve.

This stage is very much a scientific approach, one of trial and error. **It is not the answers that are important but the process by which children will attempt to solve the problem.**

"There are no first truths, only first errors."
Bachelard (French Philosopher)

Researchers like Berliner conclude the better the quality of the question the more the brain is challenged to think.

That is why open-ended questions will form the basis for the future development of children using this program.

There are in fact eight different trains (decompositions).
p = r + w + w = 4w = p = w + r + w = w + w + r = g + w = w + g = w + r + w
4 = 2 + 1 + 1 = 4 x 1 = 4 = 1 + 2 + 1 = 1 + 1 + 2 = 3 + 1 = 1 + 3 = 1 + 2 + 1

Note that children will choose to say w + w (addition) or 2w (multiplication) as they become familiar with the signs. They are simply assigning different 'names' to a particular number. More about this later.

Open questions are more challenging and allow children to progress at their own level.

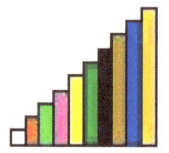

UNIT 24: Families of Equivalent Addition

FAMILIES OF EQUIVALENT ADDITION: PARTITIONS

Questions will now be use to introduce the study of partitions of length (families of equivalent addition)

*"How many trains can you make equal in length to . . .
blue;
yelllow;
dark green;
orange . . . etc.?"*

Here is what children might create in response to:

"How many trains can you make equal to the blue rod.?"

B = p + y = w + g + p + w = d + w + r
9 = 4 + 5 = 1 + 3 + 4 + 1 = 6 + 1 + 2

"How many trains can you make equal in length to . . .

orange plus red (say quickly);
orange plus dark green . . . etc.?

"How many trains can you make equal in length to . . .

three times pink;
four time light green;
five times red . . . etc.?"

There are endless possibilities.

Don't be afraid to formulate your own questions.
The more you use the material the more confident and creative you will become.

Children will approach this task as he/she would a jigsaw.

REMEMBER we are not trying to find all the 'answers' at this stage.
It is the process that is important.

As a matter of interest there are 256 possible permutations.

UNIT 25: Families of Equivalent Factors and Products

Questions that direct children to make trains of one colour equal to a given length:

"How many trains of one colour can you make equal in length to three times pink . . . two times orange . . two times orange plus pink . . . etc.

Again, these are only a few examples and you can think of many, many more.

In response to the question, "How many trains of one colour can you make equal to two times dark green?" Your child might produce :

$$2d = 3p = 4g = 6r = 12w$$
$$2 \times 6 = 3 \times 4 = 4 \times 3 = 6 \times 2 = 12 \times 1$$

This represents the complete 'table'. There are no missing pieces to this particular jigsaw. Quite possibly children will not find them all. Don't worry! At this point we are still concerned with the process not in finding every possible answer.

If we rearrange the green and pink trains into a rectangle we find that:

4 x g = 3 x p or 4g = 3p
4 x 3 = 3 x 4

This is the commutative property of addition and multiplication we will discover when children are ready to move to the next phase.

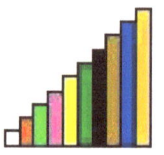# UNIT 26: Families of Equivalent Subtraction

Questions we now ask will lead to the study of families of equivalent subtraction.

We are going to compare pairs of rods/trains of differing length all of which have the same difference.

You may want to use the term 'gap' to begin with.

Once children understand what it means you can substitute the term 'difference'.

Below are some examples of pairs of rods/trains with one thing in common.

The difference between them is always equal to the pink rod.

They all belong to the same family – the family of the equivalent difference of pink (4).

y - w = p   d - r = p
5 - 1 = 4   6 - 2 = 4

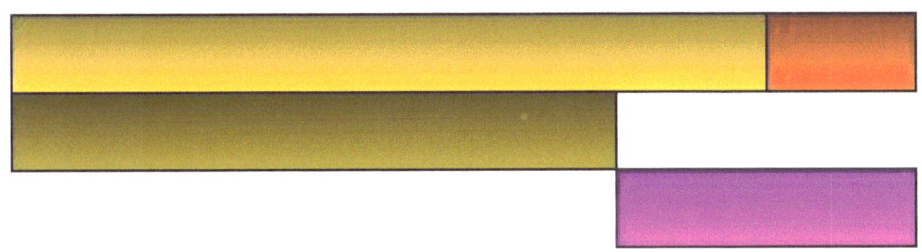

(o + r) - t = p
(10 + 2) - 8 = 4

Place two rods side by side so the difference is always equal to the pink rod . . . the red rod . . . the yellow rod . . . etc."

Now challenge children further.

Once they have found a pair with a difference of pink why not ask:

"If you add a red . . . green . . . etc. to the pair you have found will the difference still be equal to pink?"

(y + r) - (w + r) = p
7 - 3 = 4

(d + g) - (r + g) = p
9 - 5 = 4

or

p = (y + r) - (w + r) = (d + g) - (r + g) = . . .
4 = 7 - 3 = 9 - 5 = . . .

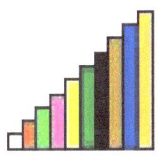

UNIT 27: Families of Equivalent Fractions

FAMILIES OF EQUIVALENT FRACTIONS (QUOTIENTS)

Start with:
r,g; _2,4

Add another red and another green:
2r, 2g; 2x2, 2x3

We now have two different lengths whose RATIO is equivalent to the first pair.

Add another red and another green:
3r, 3g; 3 x 2, 3 x 3

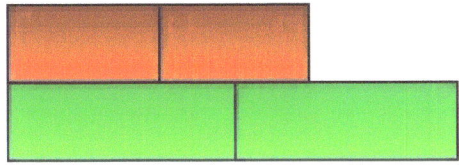

We have now created another pair of trains whose RATIO is again equivalent to the first pair.

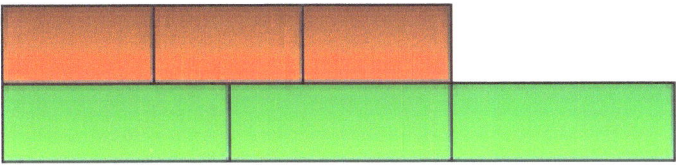

These new lengths can be substituted for rods of one colour:

r, g

2r, 2g
p, d

3r, 3g
d, B

Say:

*"Place a pair of rods side by side. Add another one of the same colour to each rod/train?
Can you change these new trains (lengths) for other rods and trains?*

Try again.

This time add two . . . three . . . four . . . (of the same colour) . . . to the first pair and change them for different lengths and trains."

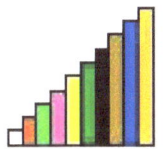 # UNIT 28: End Of Stage One

Time to stand back for a moment and review the where we've been.

Throughout this stage the main approach has been one of TRIAL and ERROR.
The GAME has been of utmost importance in creating a positive and exciting learning environment.

The main ingredient has been, and will be YOU.

TALK is of vital importance – encouraging, questioning, challenging and stimulating talk.

Because of the relationship you have with your children you are able to provide them with the quality feedback so vital to success.

FREE PLAY

Take photos/save creations from the software.
APPRECIATE and ENJOY children's creations.

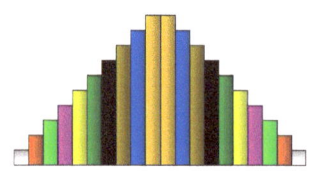

COLOUR

The power of colour – concepts learned through colour before number.

THE BIG PICTURE.

Learners should always be presented with the BIG PICTURE.

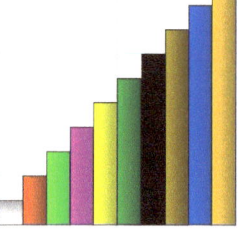

When we go on a journey by car to a strange place we refer to a map. It gives us a global overview. The BIG PICTURE is always at the back of our mind even when focusing on a specific part of the route.

Cuisenaire rods give children immediate possession of the BIG PICTURE. Each step has taken you into new, exciting challenges. You may have occasionally meandered off the planned route but you still have the BIG PICTURE to refer to.

MENTAL STIMULATION.

Play with the rods stimulates children's brains. Dr Jean Houston's work proved that stimulation of the body can stimulate the mind. Kandel and Hawkins confirmed that exercising the extremities of the body produced a positive effect on the brain.

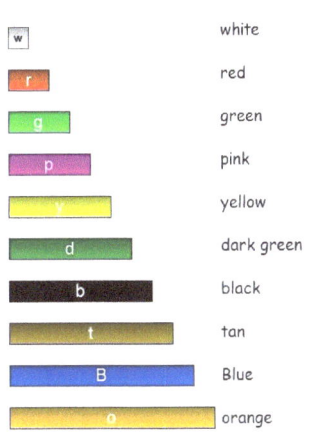

VOCABULARY

Introduction of the necessary vocabulary:

- colour names
- words and phrases
- letter names.

DIRECTED ACTIVITIES

Ask children to create something specific such as a castle or a starship.

TOUCH GAMES

Games that ensure children can visualise the rods - mental-imaging - vital for many aspects of learning and life.

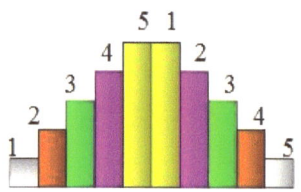

STAIRCASES

Numbering the rods (steps) going up and going down.
Increasing memory recall.

INTRODUCING SIGNS

< >   +   =   -   ×   ÷   ¼

The importance of providing as many examples as possible for each sign.
The link with language development.

READING TRAINS (math sentences/equations) together.
The 'flow'.
Children will learn to 'read' the trains and patterns (trains placed side by side with each other for comparison in a variety of new ways as new signs are introduced.

BRACKETS (PARENTHESES)

The need for brackets to avoid confusion.
The 'Say It Quick Technique'.
"*Yellow minus green* (Quickly) plus red."
Answer: pink.
"Yellow minus *green plus red* (Quickly)
Answer: 0

QUESTIONS

Questions used to generate open-ended tasks and set challenges leading to self discovery at the level of the child.
Berliner reports the better the quality of the questions asked the more the brain is challenged to think.

Questions used to intoduce basic math concepts. Such as:

- Families of Equivalent Addition.
- Families of Equivalent Products (Factors).
- Families of Equivalent Subtraction.
- Families of Equivalent Fractions (Quotients)

GAMES

Maths concepts always introduced as a game that constantly becomes more challenging.

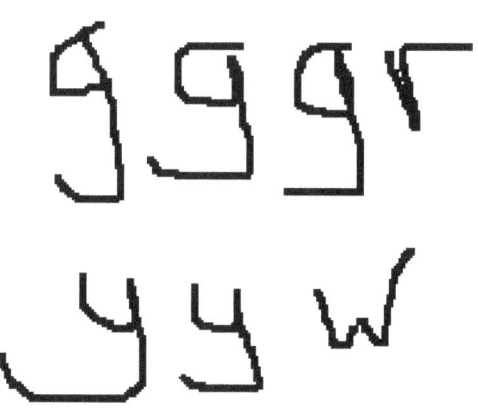

WRITING

Having been given the signs and the initial letter names children
have all they need to begin writing.
An abundance of practical experience with the rods and opportunities to 'read' their constructions should precede writing.
Once they begin writing children should do so every day.

UNIT 29: Getting Organised and Moving On

MOVING ON

Once children begin to organise their constructions into some kind of consistent pattern you know that mentally, in terms of understanding math concepts, they are moving on.

They are no longer depending on mere trial and error.

The **PATTERN** alongside is a good example.

This pattern reveals your child has discovered the **COMMUTATIVE** nature of addition.

Once the commutative nature of multiplication is also discovered children will have halved the number of table facts they needs to learn.

It does not matter that they have never heard the term 'commutative'

$y = r + g = g + r = p + w = w + p$

$5 = 2 + 3 = 3 + 2 = 4 + 1 = 1 + 4$

Another clue that children are mentally moving on is when you see this kind of pattern in their written work:

What matters is they understand the concept.

You can give it a name later!

TIP:
We want to encourage children to experiment and explore, not worry about the 'wrong' answer.

At this stage 'wrong' answers do not matter. What matters is we cultivate the natural desire to learn with which children are born.

$d = g + r + w = r + g + w = w + r + g = g + w + r =$

$6 = 3 + 2 + 1 = 2 + 3 + 1 = 1 + 2 + 3 = 1 + 2 + 3 = 3 + 1 + 2 =$

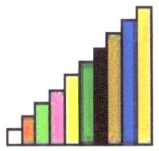# UNIT 30: 'Beyond' the Rods

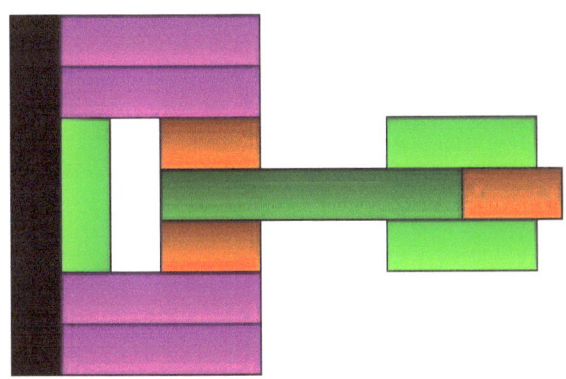

... 'To Boldly Go'...
BEYOND THE RODS

Some people use the rods as if they were a cumbersome calculating machine.
They are not.

The rods will help children move from the concrete to the abstract.

Some people think children are learning about the rods.
They are not.

Children are learning maths concepts through the rods.

Once children have grasped the concept of subtraction, for example, they will no longer

Begin to help children think 'beyond the rods' by asking questions like:
"Can you find another member of this family?"
(The family of the equivalent difference of pink/four).
d - r
6 - 2

Challenge children to try naming 'family pairs' without the rods.
Please don't allow this to become a stress situation. Stress is the enemy of learning. When we are stressed our 'thinking brain' shuts down.

When it becomes obvious they are struggling let them use the rods.

need the rods. They will rely on mental imaging to help them.

Eventually symbols- , colour, letter, number – will take their place.

Children of all ages enjoy using the rods.

The rods can easily be used to explain Pythagoras' Theorem.

They will try to find them all.

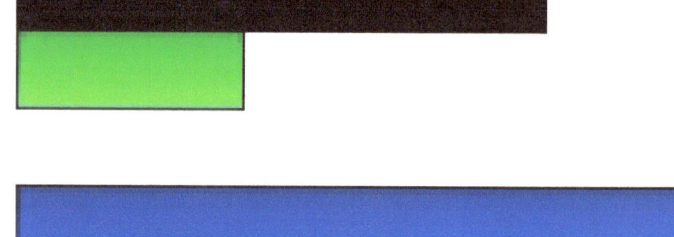

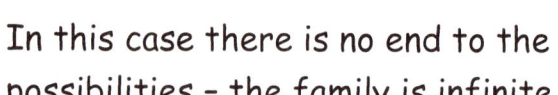

In this case there is no end to the possibilities – the family is infinite.

UNIT 31: Studying 'Families'

STUDYING FAMILIES – An Overview

Once you begin to study 'families' with the rods you will see definite patterns begin to emerge.

When writing children will refer to the rods less and less. There are good reasons for this:

Children will begin to notice that some families have distinct characteristics (properties) - just like their own!

They will begin to consciously use these properties in their written work.

They will begin to 'read' **TRAINS**, **PATTERNS** (trains placed side by side) and **MATS** (several trains placed side by side) in a variety of ways.

TRAINS

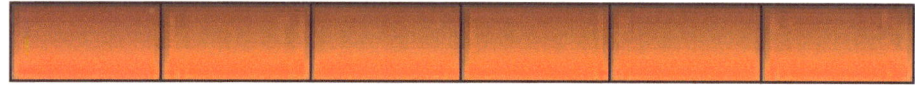

r + r + r + r + r + r = 6r = 2r + 2r + 2r = 3r + 3r =

2 + 2 + 2 + 2 + 2 + 2 = 6 × 2 = (2 × 2) + (2 × 2) + (2 × 2) = (3 × 2) + (3 × 2) =

Families of factors or divisors.

MATS

The signs children have used are: =   +   ×   ( )

o + r = r + r + r + r + r + r = 6r = (r + r) + (r + r) + (r + r) = p + p + p = 3p = (r + r + r) + (r + r + r) = d + d = 2d

12 = 2 + 2 + 2 + 2 + 2 + 2 = 6 × 2 = (2 + 2) + (2 + 2) + (2 + 2) = 4 + 4 + 4 = 3 × 4 = (2 + 2 + 2) + (2 + 2 + 2) = 6 + 6 = 2 × 6

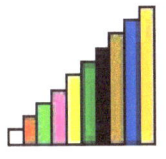# UNIT 32: Families of Partitions (Length)

TABLES OF PARTITIONS OF LENGTH.

While studying the previous MAT an important discovery has been made:
Permutations of the rods in any one train leads to the discovery of a new partition.

In the example below we shall once again employ the '**SAY IT QUICK TECHNIQUE'** – great for auditory and visual learners.

'SAY IT QUICK'

Children quickly grasp the concept of creating new partitions using this method. What they in fact do is 'bracket' the rods you repeat quickly together mentally. Then, applying mental imagery, they replace the rods with one length.

For example:

"Red plus red."

"Red plus red plus red."

The possibilities are endless. Always provide the children with plenty of encouragement and praise.

UNIT 33: Tables of Partitions Without the Rods

TABLES OF PARTITIONS WITHOUT THE RODS.

This time try the previous examples without the rods.

You might say:

"Try this without the rods. I am going to read a train. Which two colours am I adding together?"

Read any train that springs to mind:
e g *"Yellow plus red plus green."*

$y + r + g$
$5 + 2 + 3$

Say, "**yellow plus red,**" quickly.

$(y + r) + g$
$b + g$
$(5 + 2) + 3$
$7 + 3$

Your child should say "**black** *plus green*"

This time say "**red plus green**" quickly.

$y + (r + g)$
$y + y$
$5 + (2 + 3)$
$5 + 5$

Your child should now read "yellow plus yellow".

As always provide plenty of examples.
Children have now discovered the associative property of addition. Another family characteristic!

Try these with your children:

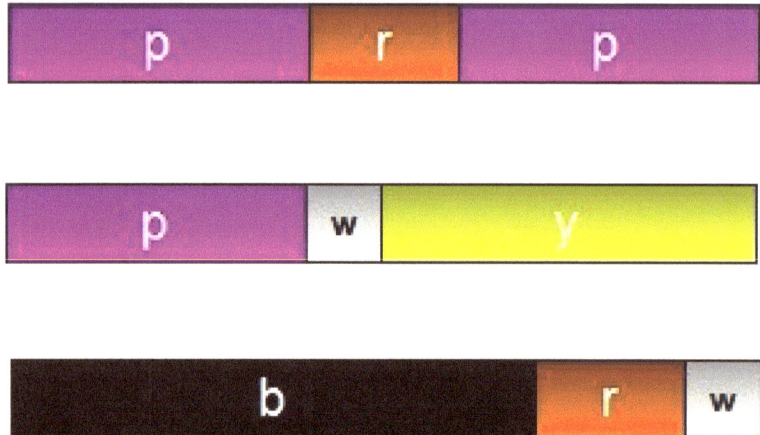

Each challenge is also unconsciously reinforcing number bonds to 10.

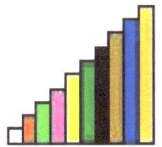

UNIT 34: Time Out for Talk.

THE IMPORTANCE OF POSITIVE TALK

"As a man thinks in his heart, so he is."
Solomon (10th CENTURY BC)

"You are today where your thoughts have brought you; you will be tomorrow where your thoughts take you."
James Allen (1849-1925) American Author

Today's self-motivation gurus are only repeating truths that have been expressed in different forms down the centuries.

It is frightening that in a very real way we are the authors of our own destiny.
Walking self-fulfilling prophecies.

TIME OUT!

This section is for ADULTS ONLY

Words affect the way we think and act.
They affect our emotional state, the single most important state for learning.
There are words we can use to activate our children's abilities.
We can, by use of language, literally choose which ability to activate. If we model positive talk our children will unconsciously copy it.
Your child will reap the emotional, physical and spiritual benefit. Phrases that have a powerful and positive impact are:

"Yes" . . . "Yes but..! . . .

"Yes when..! . . .

"That's wonderful..!". . .

"That's interesting..!". . .

"Imagine..!" . . .

It is vital we teach our children to take control of their thoughts. So many of our actions are based on habits that spring from deep within our sub-conscious.

How do they get there? We put them there ourselves or allow others to do so.

Children need to be nurtured in a positive environment. Self-esteem is the well spring of motivation. It is self-motivated people who grab life by the lapels and make things happen.

Our sub-conscious accepts what it is told. We need to be very careful of what seeds we sow in our children's minds.

"Imagine you are..." . . .

"That's unusual..!. . .

"I admire the way you..." . . .

"Ah Yes!..!" . . .

"I am feeling..." . . .

"Feel..!" . . .

This is a whole learning area in itself but if we can teach our children to feel good about themselves, if we can show them how to talk themselves up, then they will handle the inevitable put-downs life throws our way. Peoples' lives frequently turn on a thoughtless, callous or ignorant remark that is allowed to penetrate deep into their being.

That's tragic.

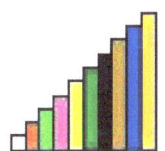

UNIT 35: The Commutative Property of Addition

The Cummutative Property of Addition

Children have now met the associative property of addition. We now focus on questions that highlight the commutative property (characteristic) of addition. Once children have fully grasped these two concepts they will be better equipped to gather facts in a more organised way.

"Choose any rod longer than pink. Can you make a train of (three . . . four . . . five . . . etc.) equal to it?"

Give children time to complete the task.

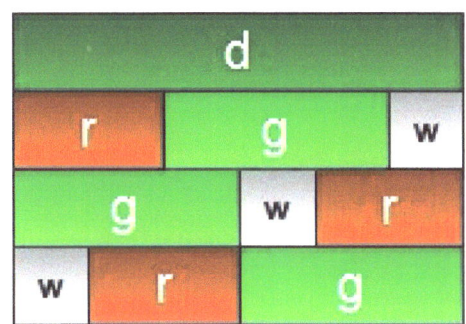

$d = r + g + w = g + w + r = w + r + g$
$6 = 2 + 3 + 1 = 3 + 1 + 2 = 1 + 2 + 3$

"Does it matter which order I put the rods in the train?
Will they still equal the dark green (black, tan, Blue, orange . . . etc.)"

TIP
Take time to play games children have already mastered. It is always good to confirm and affirm what we already know. It also builds self-esteem.

"In a world that is constantly changing, there is no one subject or set of subjects that will serve you for the foreseeable future, let alone for the rest of your life. The most important skill to acquire now is learning how to learn."

John Naisbitt - Futurist

Provide plenty of examples until children are convinced that, no matter what order the rods are placed, they will always equal the dark green.

Try the same challenge for:

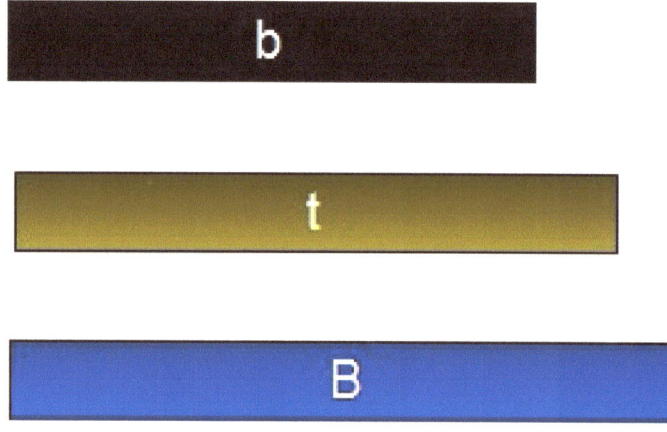

UNIT 36: Studying 'Families'.

MENTAL SUBSTITUTION

Play games that consolidate what has already been learnt before increasing the challenge.

Tell children you are going to hold up a rod that is less than orange(10).
They must quickly hold up the rod that,
added to yours, equals orange.

This is good practice in consolidating number bonds.

If children are confident in their response, increase the challenge. Tell them to close their eyes and this time you will simply name the rod. They must respond orally without looking at or touching the rods.

When the number names of the rods are introduced children will have no problem recalling number bonds to 10 instantly.
No fingers needed!

Now extend the game to ensure children have a secure grasp of the associative and commutative properties of addition.

"Name a train of 3 (4, 5 . . .) rods equal to orange . . . blue . . . etc."
"Imagine you have mixed up the rods in the train. Put them back in a different order and name them."
"Close your eyes and imagine your train. Now change two of the rods for just one and read the train again."

The ability to substitute mentally is very important. Often the 'family' is just too large so children must learn to start with the simplest examples and test whether what they have discovered holds good in more complex situations. For example when considering partitions of the rods start with white and work up.

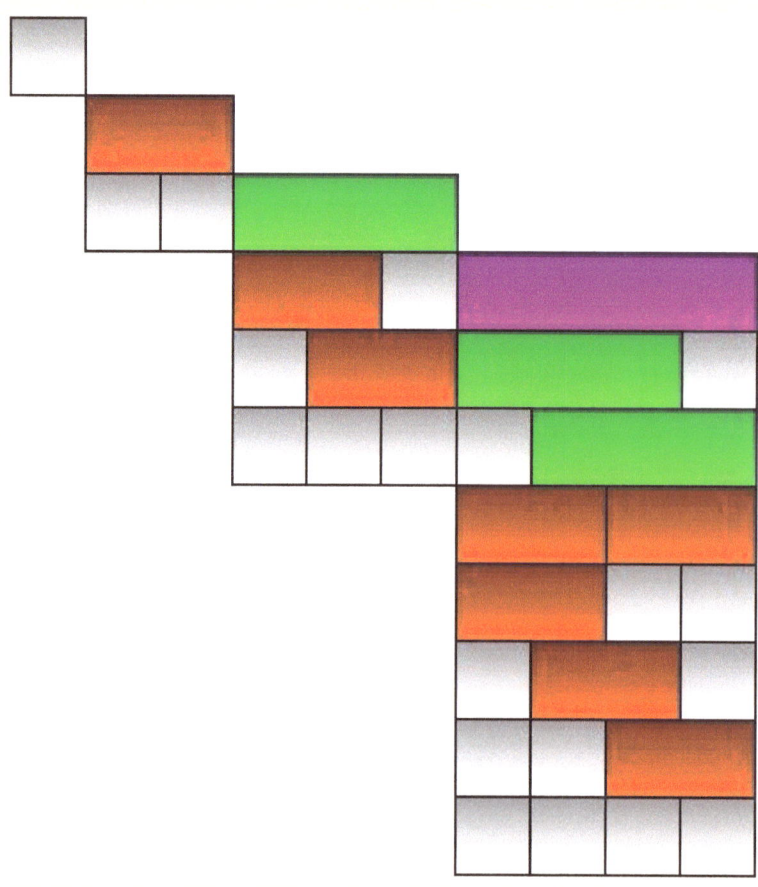

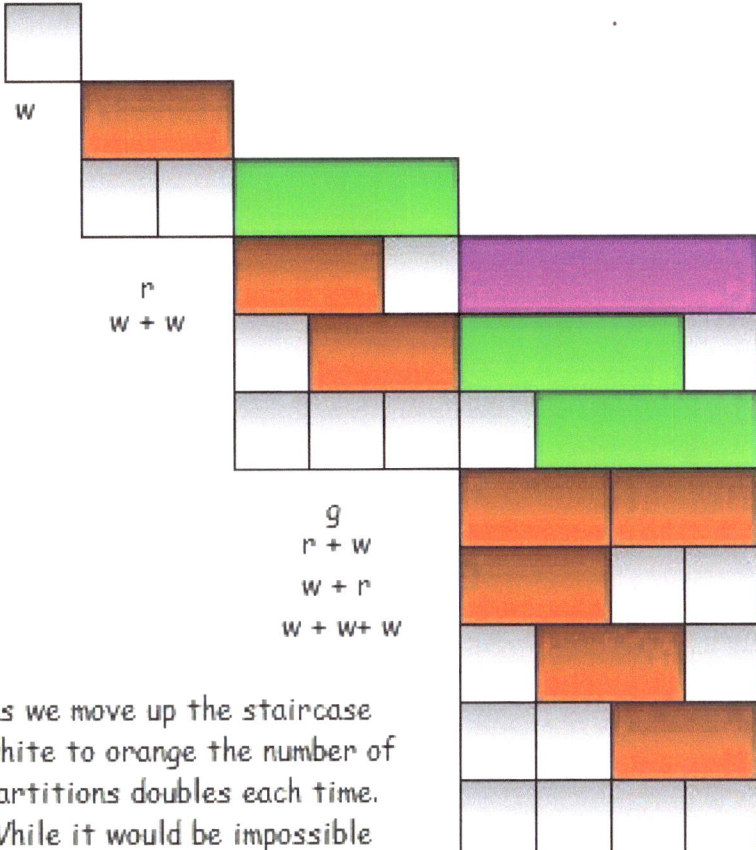

w

r
w + w

g
r + w
w + r
w + w + w

As we move up the staircase white to orange the number of partitions doubles each time. While it would be impossible for children to find all the the possible partitions for, say orange (512 partitions), they can now estimate, based on what they have already discovered, all the possible partitions of any given rod.

p
g + w
w + g
r + r
r + w + w
w + r + w
w + w + r
w + w + w + w

UNIT 37: The 'Grain of Rice' Principle.

We all know the story of the grain of rice and the chessboard.

We find the same principle at work when we partition the rods.

Moving from orange (10) to orange plus white (11) the number of partitions doubles from 512 to 1,024.

If we were using the rods like some crude calculating machine we would have reached saturation point by now.

It is worth restating that what the rods do is free the mind to think for itself.

There comes a point where the rods are consciously

Once children have found all the possible partitions of orange using just two rods each time we can re-arrange them in a particular order.

```
    o     10
  B + w   9 + 1
  t + r   8 + 2
  b + g   7 + 3
  d + p   6 + 4
```

placed to one side in favour of abstract thought processes that the rods have helped develop.

At this stage you would probably agree with children that attempting to find all the possible partitions of orange is too difficult.

Instead ask:

"What if we find all the trains (lengths) equal to orange using just two rods each time."

This is very familiar territory we can explore afresh to examine new concepts.

y + y   5 + 5
p + d   4 + 6
g + b   3 + 7
r + t   2 + 8
w + o   1 + 9

This is an example of compensatory dynamics at work where one side
decreases in length while the other increases.

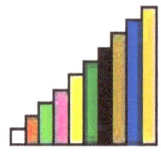# UNIT 38: Free Expression.

As we start to take a closer look at each 'family' you will find children's free writing will result in a greater variety of expression. They will use mental substitution to move from simple to more complex equations.

Children will delight in making long and complicated looking equations – especially if you look suitably impressed!

Remember though, practical experience (play) and lots of mental work in the form of games and questions comes before writing.

Take this train as an example:

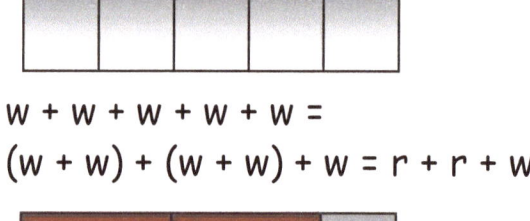

$w + w + w + w + w =$
$(w + w) + (w + w) + w = r + r + w$

The **associative property** of addition.

Para 315 ... Young children should not be allowed to move too quickly to written work in mathematics. It follows that, in the early stages, mental and oral work should form a major part of the mathematics which is done. As a child grows older, he needs to begin to develop the methods of mental calculation which he will use throughout his life ...

... although it is possible to practice written methods of computation as routines with little understanding of the underlying method, good mental methods have to be based on understanding ...

... to extend mathematical insights without the added of formal recording.

**Dr W.H.Cockroft
Mathematics Counts
(HMSO 1982)**

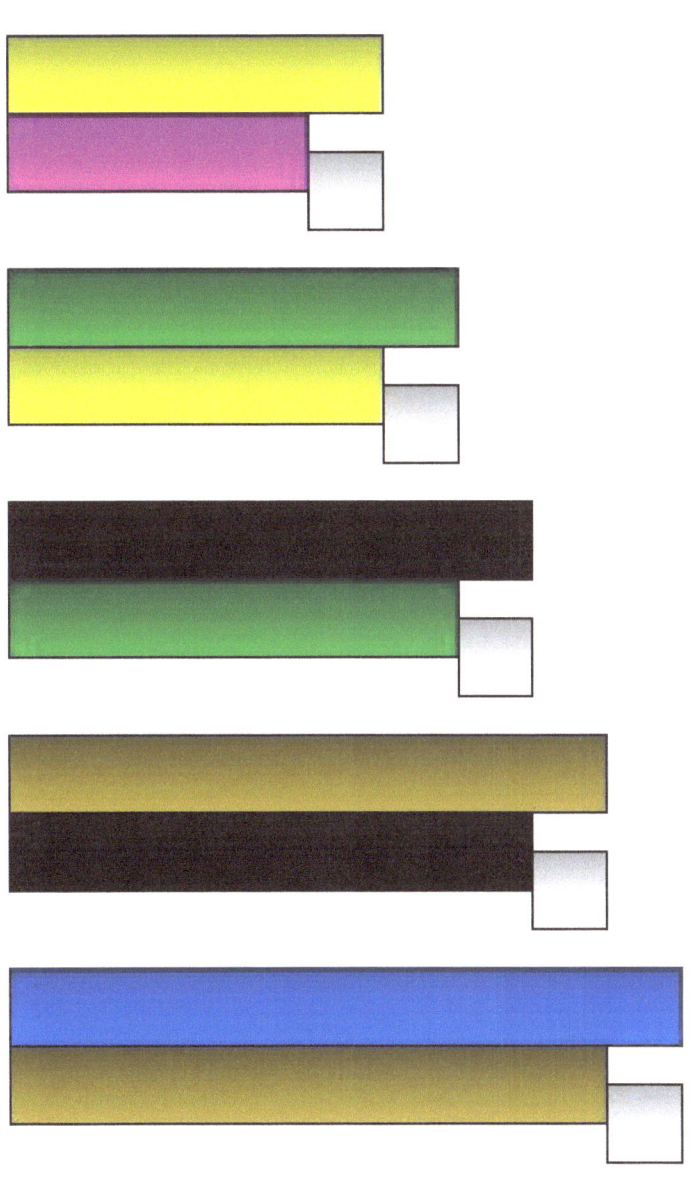

$(y - p) + (d - y) + (b - d) + (t - b) + (B - t)$
Families of **equivalent difference**.

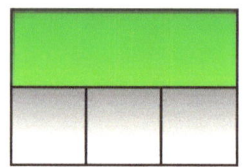

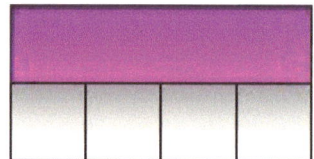

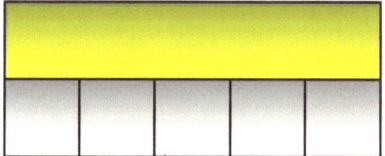

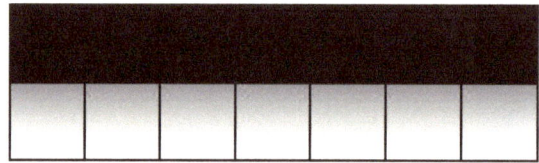

(1/3 × g) + (1/4 × p) + (1/7 × b) + (1/8 × t) + (1/5 × y)

Fractions as operators..

As a numerical equation it would look like this:
1 + 1 + 1 + 1 + 1 = (1 + 1) + (1 + 1) + 1 = 2 + 2 + 1 = (5 − 4) + (6 − 5) + (7 − 6) + (8 − 7) + (9 − 8) = (1/3 × 3) + (1/4 × 4) + (1/5 × 5) + (1/6 × 6) + (1/7 × 7) . . . etc.

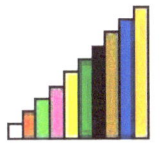

UNIT 39: Families of Equivalent Difference.

FAMILIES OF EQUIVALENT DIFFERENCE – A CLOSER LOOK

Ask, "*Is pink equal to yellow?*"

"*No,*" (hopefully),

"*What would I have to do to yellow to make it equal to pink?*"

Give prompts if needed.
e g "*Is yellow bigger or smaller than pink? Should I add or subtract?*"

Because yellow is bigger than pink children will probably reply, "*Subtract*".

Ask, "*Subtract what?*"

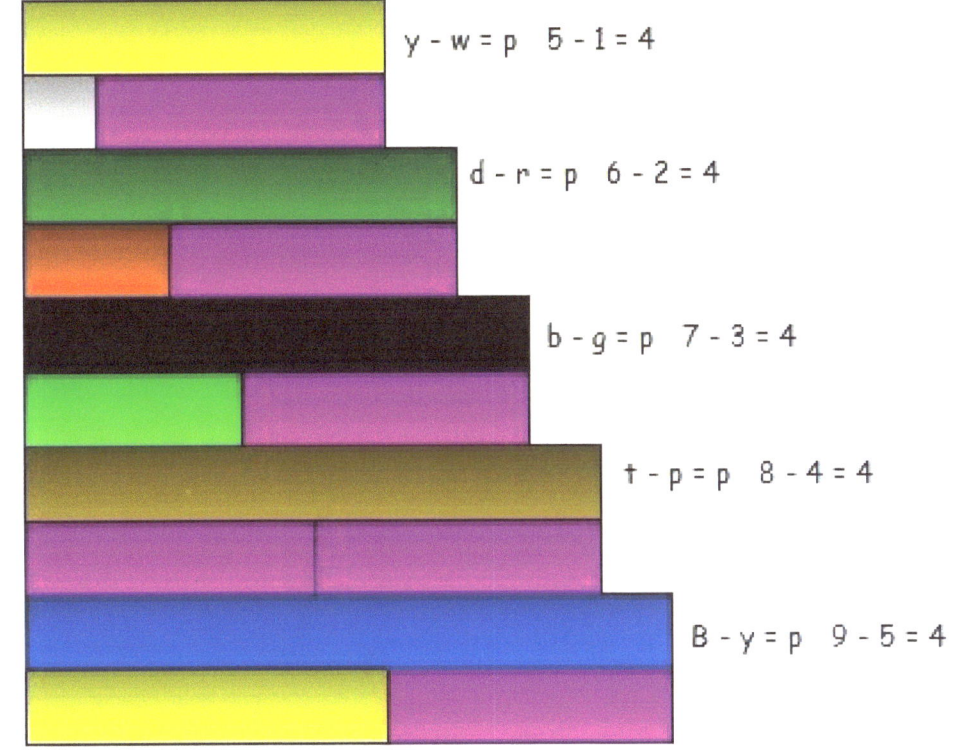

$y - w = p \quad 5 - 1 = 4$

$d - r = p \quad 6 - 2 = 4$

$b - g = p \quad 7 - 3 = 4$

$t - p = p \quad 8 - 4 = 4$

$B - y = p \quad 9 - 5 = 4$

We can arrange the rods into two staircases that show this progression more clearly. Children should be able to predict the next step in each staircase.

They will more than likely have already told you subtract white. Now ask, "*Is pink equal to dark green?*"

Follow the same process.

Continue with the subsequent steps in the staircase, black, tan, Blue and orange.

Children should begin to notice a logical progression. This can be written as :

p = y − w = d − r = b − g = t − p = B − y = o − d . . .
4 = 5 − 1 = 6 − 2 = 7 − 3 = 8 − 4 = 9 − 5 = 10 − 6

We are now ready to extend the challenge,

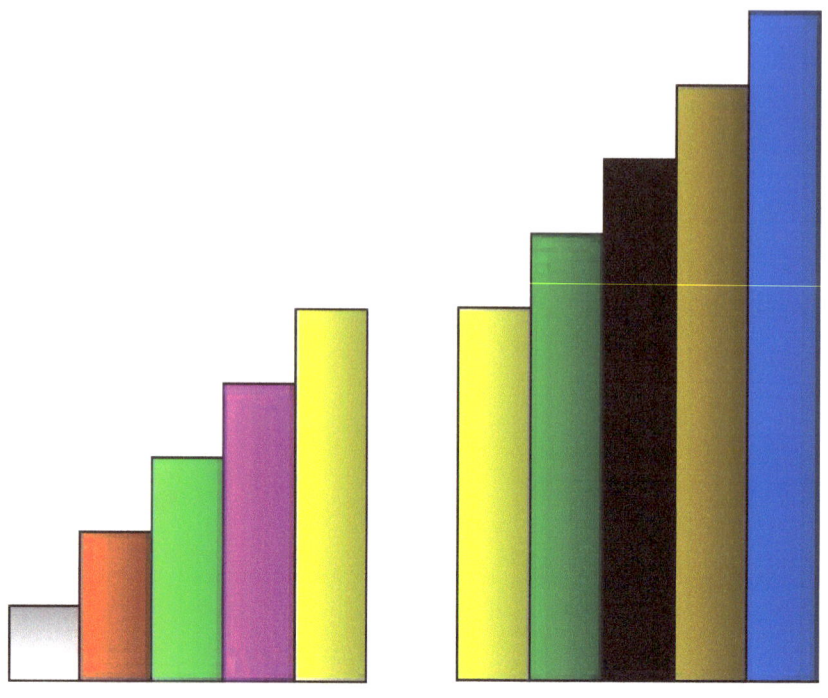

UNIT 40: Extending the Challenge

FAMILIES OF EQUIVALENT DIFFERENCE
– Extending the Challenge

Using the same example children should now be able to name with confidence the next member of the family.

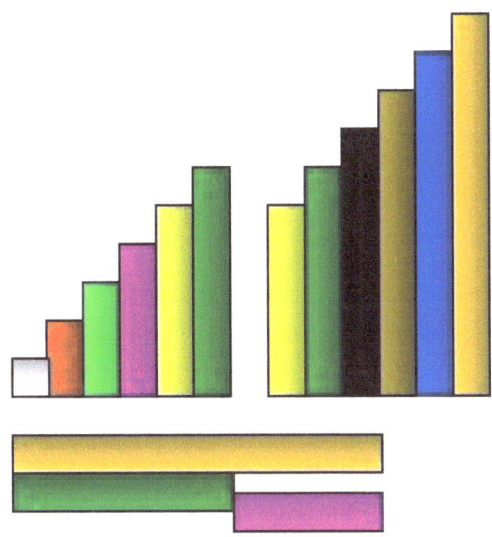

Could children reproduce this pattern for other members of the family of equivalent difference, say red, green etc?

"Can you find the eighth member of this family?"

If you think children are ready extend the challenge.

"Can you find it without using the rods?"

Try this approach for the family of equivalent difference equal to black(7) . . . dark green (8) . . . etc.

Other arrangements of the same rods are possible:

$y - w = p = (w + y) - r = d - r = (r + y) - g = b - g = (g + y) - p = t - p =$ etc.

$5 - 1 = 4 = (1 + 5) - 2 = 6 - 2 = (2 + 5) - 3 = 7 - 3 = (3 + 5) - 4 = 8 - 4$ etc.

These can be arranged to form a very interesting pattern children will feel able to continue.

UNIT 41: Families of Factors/Divisors

FAMILIES OF FACTORS AND DIVISORS

Remember we are opening children's eyes to the rich and vibrant landscape of math where patterns can be discovered and observed with every fresh challenge

   As before say:

"Make a train using rods of only one colour.
Now make a train equal to it, again, using rods of one colour."

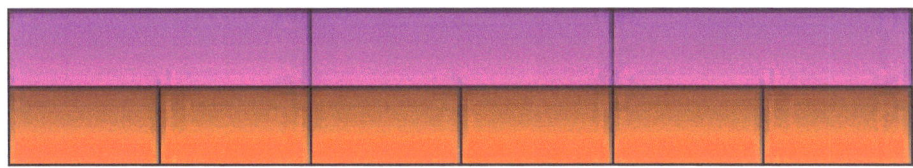

This will probably be quite a simple task as children have now accomplished this many times before during
FREE PLAY and DIRECTED ACTIVITIES and during our first look at FAMILIES.

"Now place the rods in the train side by side."

 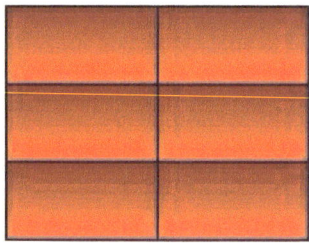

p + p + p = r + r + r + r + r + r = (r + r) + (r + r) + (r + r) = 3 × 2r = 3p

4 + 4 + 4 = 2 + 2 + 2 + 2 + 2 + 2 =

(2 + 2) + (2 + 2) + (2 + 2) = 3 × 4

Play this game until children are confident.
Again, you will probably find they grasp it very quickly because it is something that has already been observed while working with the rods.

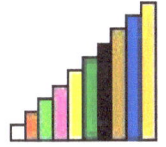

UNIT 42: Factor Families - The Commutative Property of Multiplication

FAMILIES OF FACTORS AND DIVISORS

The Commutative Property of Multiplication.

"Make a train of one colour.

Place the rods side by side to form a rectangle.

What colour rod would you now place across the (pink) rectangle to fit exactly?"

In this case the answer is green.

"Can you make a rectangle of green rods that would exactly cover the pink rods?
What colour rod would you now place across the green rectangle to fit exactly."

$$3 \times p = 4 \times g$$
$$3p = 4g$$
$$3 \times 4 = 4 \times 3$$

This can be represented by two crosses and is an example of the commutative property of multiplication.

By understanding the commutative property children will have halved the number facts they need to learn.

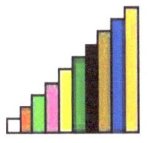

UNIT 43: Factor Families - Consolidation

FAMILIES OF FACTORS AND DIVISORS

Review and consolidation.

"Try this (the previous challenge) again with longer trains of the same colour or different colour trains."

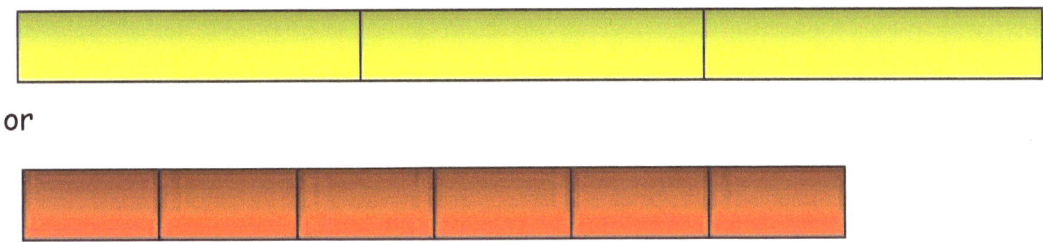

The "crosses" represent factors of a number.

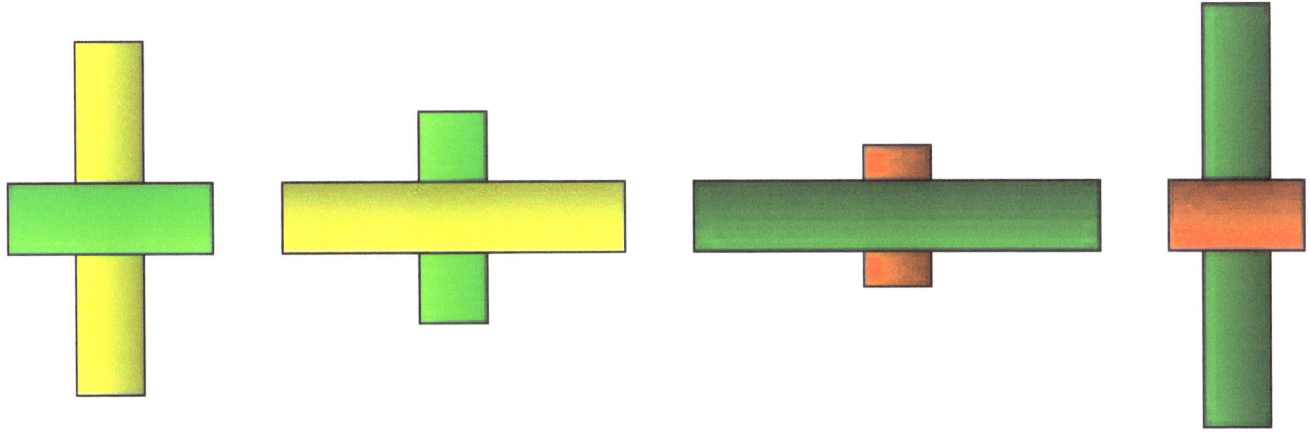

This type of work is an excellent foundation for understanding how to calculate area of regular and irregular shapes.

It is also excellent preparation for learning 'tables', a chore made far easier by the impact colour has on memory recall. What children may be led to discover is a compensating dynamic where the factors and divisors go in pairs, the smallest with the largest and so on, creating equivalent rectangles as below.

1(o + r), 2d, 3p, 4g 6r 12w

1 x 12 = 2 x 6 = 3 x 4 = 4 x 3 = 6 x 2 = 12 x 1

UNIT 44: Factor Families

FAMILIES OF FACTORS AND DIVISORS

Factors go in pairs.

You can help children see that factors of a number go in pairs by deliberately choosing certain lengths/numbers.

"Make a train of two orange plus red (24), three orange plus dark green (36), one orange plus tan (18) etc. How many trains of one colour can you make equal to orange plus red . . . ?"

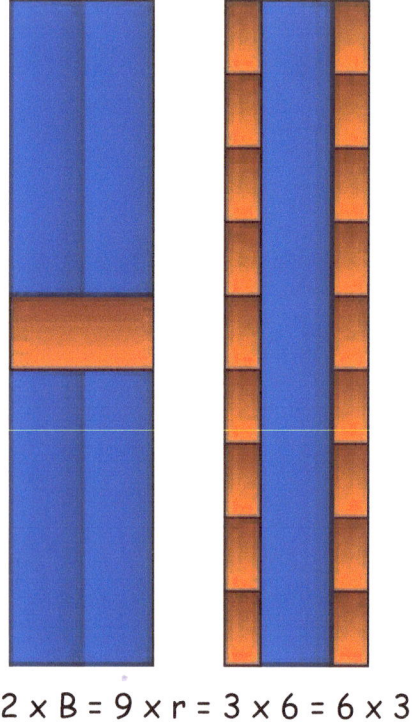

2 x B = 9 x r = 3 x 6 = 6 x 3

= 2B = 9r = 3d = 6g

= 2 x 9 = 9 x 2 = 3 x 6 = 6 x 3

These kinds of games offer an opportunity to consider fractions as operators.

UNIT 45: Numbers Have Names

FRACTIONS AS OPERATORS

Numbers can have more than one name.

Talk about your family. Choose one member, say Grandpa. Ask how many names Grandpa has. What do you call him? What does Grandma call him? What do his friends call him? What do the neighbours call him? Firmly establish that one person can have lots of names.

Because orange plus dark green is equal to two tans we can say:
$$t = 1/2 \times (o + d)$$
Because orange plus dark green is equal to four pinks we can say:
$$p = 1/4 \times (o + d)$$
Because orange plus dark green is equal to eight reds we can say:
$$r = 1/8 \times (o + d)$$
Being really clever we can compare other trains:

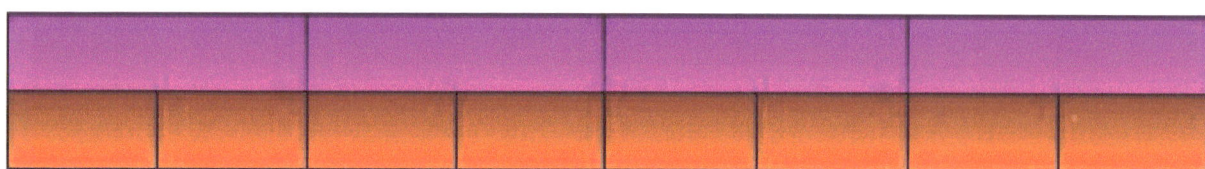

Because pink equals two reds we can say: r = 1/2 x p
We have now found two 'names' for red: r = 1/8 x (o + d) = 1/2 x p
                                    2 = 1/8 x 16 = 1/2 x 4
Using the above example there is yet another 'name' for red.
Because red is four times smaller than tan we can say: r = 1/4 x t
In reality the number of names for green, or 3, is infinite.
These 'name games' lead us naturally to the next family.

UNIT 46: Families of Equivalent Fractions/Quotients

FAMILIES OF EQUIVALENT FRACTIONS OR QUOTIENTS

Having practiced comparing rods during the 'name games' offer children a new challenge.

"Place any two rods side by side with the biggest underneath."

"Imagine this is the first step in the light green staircase and dark green is the first step in the dark green staircase. What would the next steps be?"

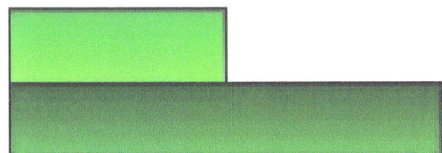

"Can you replace the light greens with a single rod?"

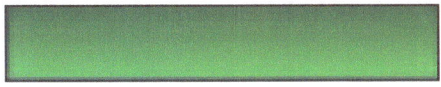

"Can you replace the two dark greens for a single rod?" (The answer this time is no but suggest another train beginning with orange.)

This is now the second member of the family: (g, d) (d, o + r)

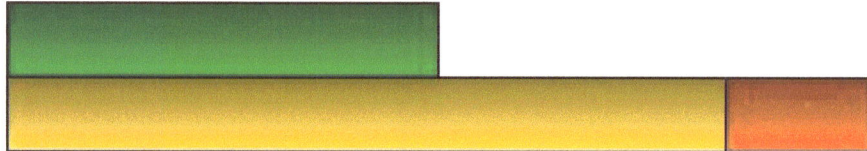

"Try and find the third member of the family."

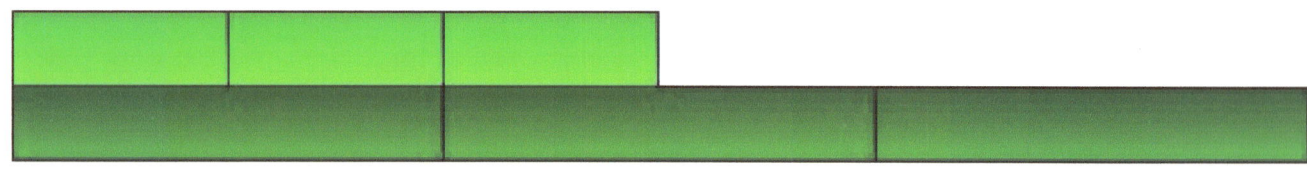

We now have: (g, d), (d, o + r), (B, o + t)...
        3/6,   6/12,   9/18 ...

UNIT 47: Equivalent Fraction Families - Generating Staircases

FAMILIES OF EQUIVALENT FRACTIONS AND QUOTIENTS

Generating Giant Staircases.

Let children find as many members of a particular family as he/she likes. Now say:

"Arrange the smaller/bigger rods/trains in each pair into a staircase."

These represent two sequences of numbers increasing by the length of the first rod of each number pair sequence. In this case light green and dark green.

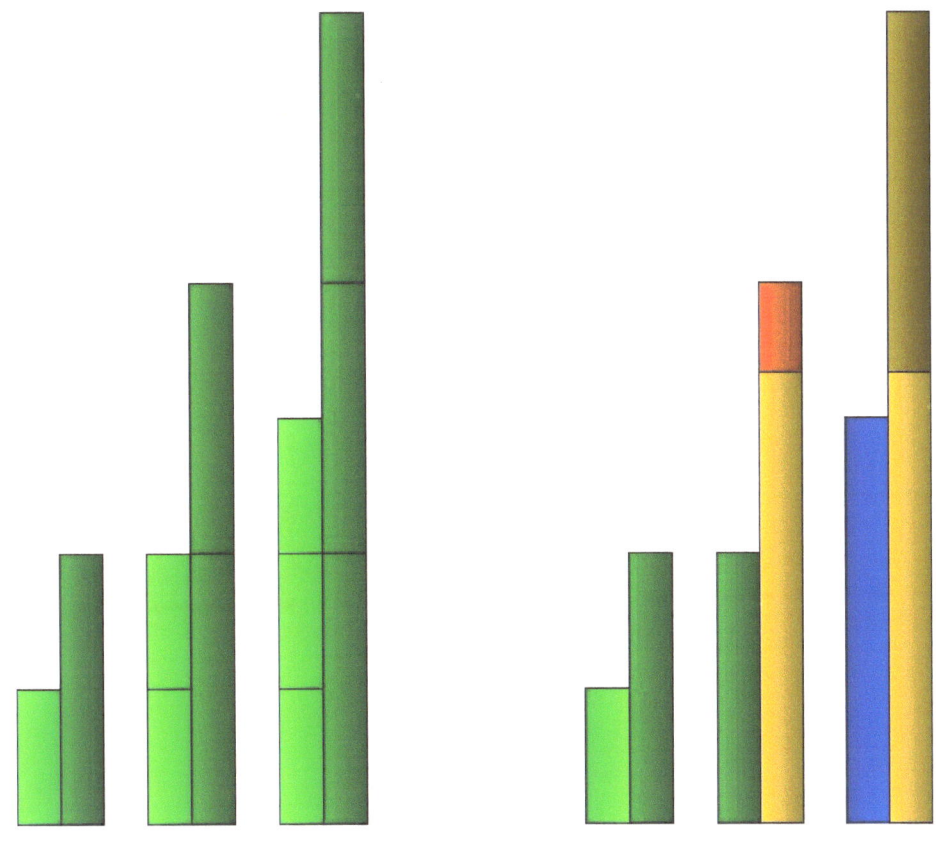

They are also the difference between each corresponding step (see below).

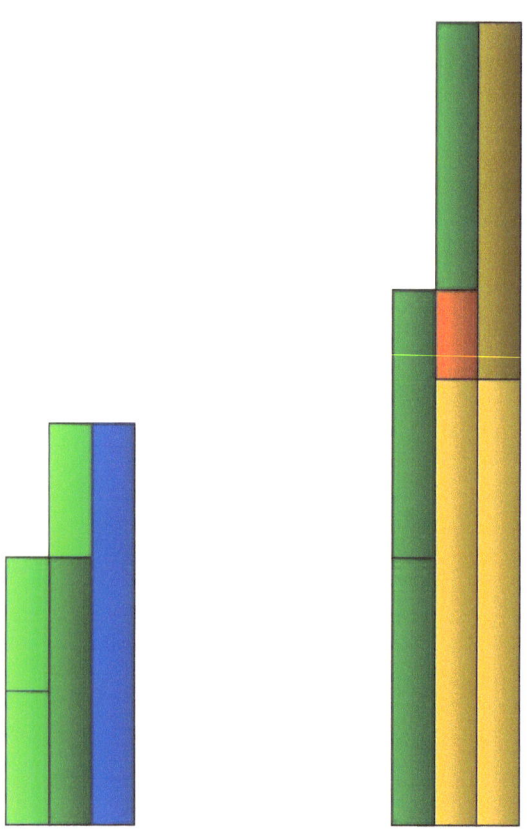

WARNING! Children could end up with a huge staircase. They delight in this activity so keep your camera handy. This is what the sequence would look like using letter and number names:

g, d = d, (o + r) = B, (o + t), = (o + r), (2o + p) = etc

3/6 = 6/12 = 9/18 = 12/24 = etc

Challenge children to try this with different pairs of rods, such as:

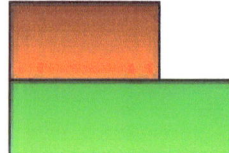  

UNIT 48: Reciprocal Fractions

FAMILIES OF EQUIVALENT FRACTIONS AND QUOTIENTS

 Generating Reciprocal Fractions.

Challenge children further.
"Place the bigger of the pair of rods on top. This is called a reciprocal fraction."

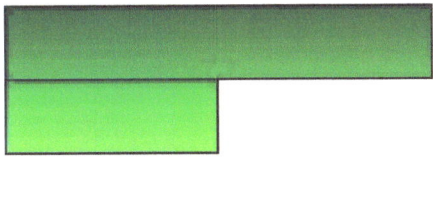

d, g = (o + r), d = (o + t), B = . . .
6/3 = 12/6 = 18/9 = . . .
This is the family equivalent to red or 2.

Once again the challenge is to find more members of the family.
This is exactly the same process except that, this time the bigger staircase is generated first.

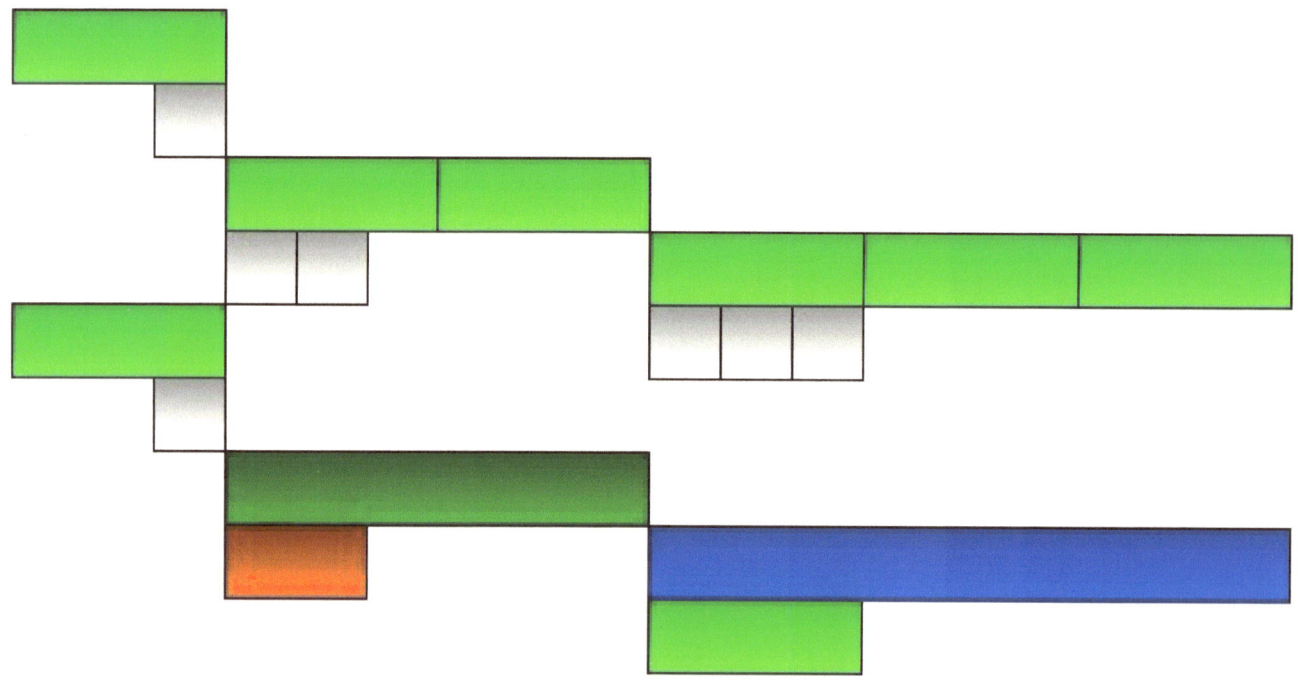

g = g, w = d, r = B, g = 3 = 3/1 = 6/2 = 9/3 = . . . etc

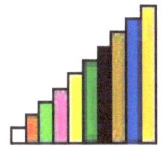

UNIT 49: The Importance of Review

REVIEWING WHERE WE'VE BEEN

REVIEWING is a vital element of learning. Every now and again we should stop to review what has been learnt. A suggested guide line for review that is used as a principle for 'accelerated' learning would be:

1. At the end of a session with the rods when a new concept has been introduced ask plenty of questions as suggested in the program.

2. The following day (morning preferably because the brain processes information it has absorbed the previous day while we sleep).

3. Review the same concept after a week.
4. Review after 1 month.
5. Review after 6 months.

It is estimated that this could increase recall by up to 4 times.
REMEMBER Learning = Understanding + Memory

Time to pause again and reflect on what we've covered since our last review.

FAMILIES

A closer look at their distinct characteristics (properties).
Equivalent addition;
The associative property;
The 'say it quick' technique;
The commutative property.

Mental Substitution – Making sure of number bonds - finding family members – families of: equivalent difference, factors and divisors – halving table facts – crosses and commutativity – preparation for area; smallest and largest – compensatory dynamics.

Numbers have names too! - fractions as operators; the 'name game' - equivalent fractions and quotients; reciprocal fractions; an introduction to integers.

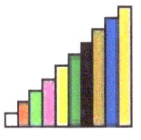 # UNIT 50: Looking Forward

LOOKING FORWARD

 The Big Picture

So far your child has passed through a number of stages. We can describe them as :

- FREE PLAY
- TRIAL & ERROR
- GETTING ORGANISED

    Next door neighbours – finding family members directly bigger or smaller

Now we want the freedom to able to go from one member of the family to any other.

Most of the streets where our families live never end. Pity the poor postman!

But these are the best streets down which children should be free to explore.

To help them achieve this level of independence we shall lean upon one particular relative within the family – equivalence.

We know the equivalence relationship is both SYMMETRICAL and TRANSITIVE
e g p = p = 2r = r + w + w = 1/3 x (o + r) = . . .
     4 = 4 = 2 x 2 = 2 + 1 + 1 = 1/3 x 12 = . . .

"So?"
All this means is that from one member of the family you can reach any other.
Just like genes, one member contains the potential to produce any other member.
Let's go meet the family

UNIT 51: Families of Equivalent Difference

 A Game to Play

Let's look at a family we have already met – the family of equivalent difference equal to pink.
Begin by choosing a member of the family.

B - y
9 - 5

"Choose any other member of the family."
Although the family is infinite children will choose a member with either a bigger or smaller pair of rods.

b - g
7 - 3

or

o - d
10 - 6

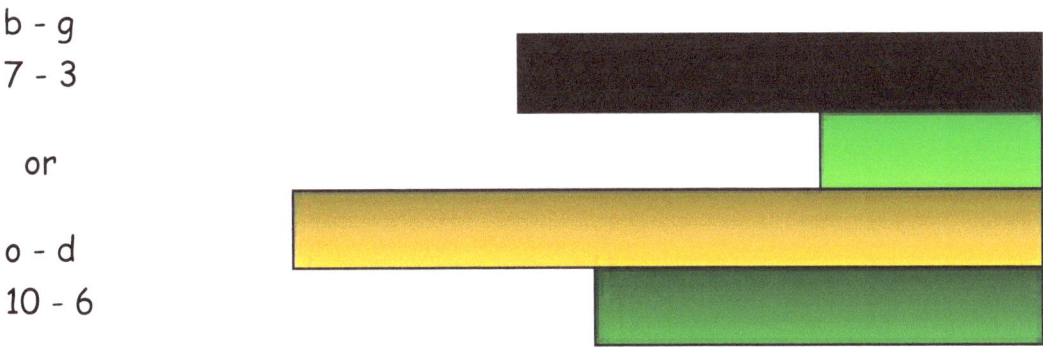

"Can you get to my family member from yours?"
If children choose a member whose pair of rods was smaller, what they must do is increase each rod by adding (compensatory dynamics):

B − y = (b + r) − (g + r)

9 − 5 = (7 + 2) − (3 + 2)

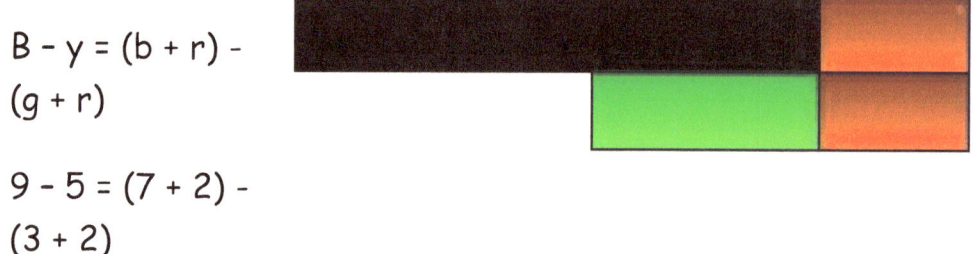

If children chooses a member whose pair of rods was bigger what they must do is reduce each rod by subtraction (compensatory dynamics):

B − y = (o − w) − (d − w)

9 − 5 = (10 − 1) − (6 − 1)

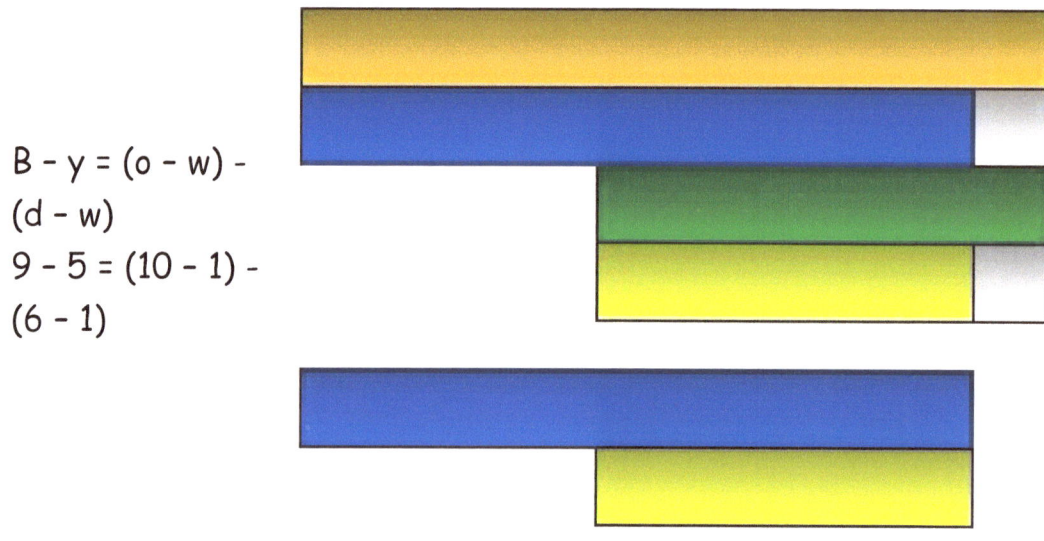

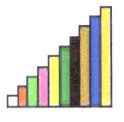# UNIT 52: Families of Equivalent Fractions - Bigger Members

FAMILIES OF EQUIVALENT FRACTIONS
As with all new developments games will be the force that drives children to further insights and discoveries.

In this game we will discover how repeated addition (iteration) will help us reach any member of the family bigger than our original pair of rods or trains, for example:

r, g = 3r, 3g

2, 3 = 3 x 2, 3 x 3,

2/3 = 6/9

Say, "Choose any pair of rods (side by side). Let's see if we can find other members of the family."

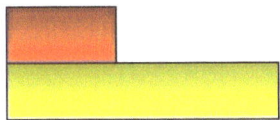

Increase one of the lengths by iteration (repeated addition).

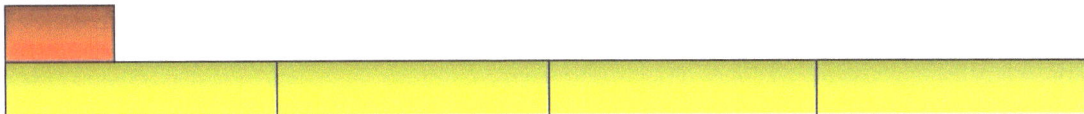

Now ask: "Can you do the same to the red rod?"

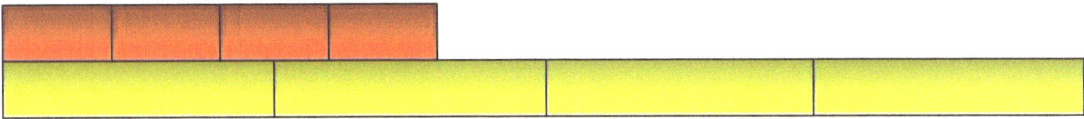

If children don't grasp it straight away try more examples until either they are sure or, if they still don't understand leave it for another time.
Treat it as a game.
Say, "Can you put a rod or rods in place of the two trains?"

r, y = 4r, 4y
2/5 = 8/20

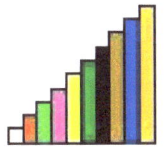

UNIT 53: Families of Equivalent Fractions - Smaller Members

FAMILIES OF EQUIVALENT FRACTIONS
From bigger to smaller.

Now challenge children to find another member of the family smaller than the one you begun with, for example:

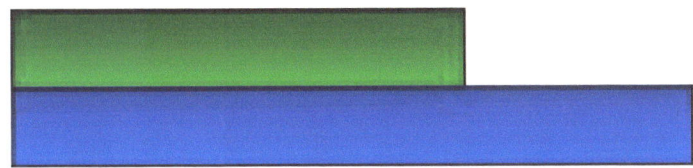

Ask, "Can you make a train of only one colour equal in length to the dark green rod?"

There are two possible solutions (excluding the white rod):

$d = r + r + r = 3r = g + g = 2g$

$6 = 2 + 2 + 2 = 3 \times 2 = 3 + 3 = 2 \times 3$

Once children have found them ask:

"Can you do the same for the blue rod?"

This time there is only one possible solution.

B = g + g + g = 3g

9 = 3 + 3 + 3 = 3 × 3

"Now choose the train for dark green and the train for blue that both have the same number of rods."

"Place them side by side."
Remove one rod from each train."

Children found this member of the family by repeated subtraction (division).

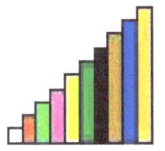

UNIT 54: Families of Equivalent Fractions - Adam and Eve

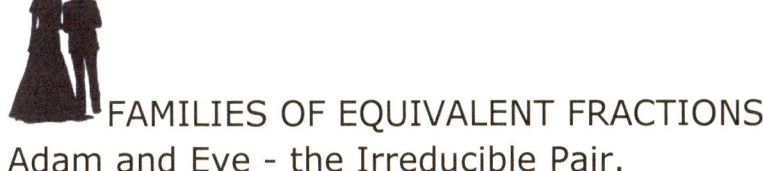

FAMILIES OF EQUIVALENT FRACTIONS
Adam and Eve - the Irreducible Pair.

Say,
"Instead of taking away one rod what would have happened if you took away two rods from each train?"
Using the example from Unit 53:

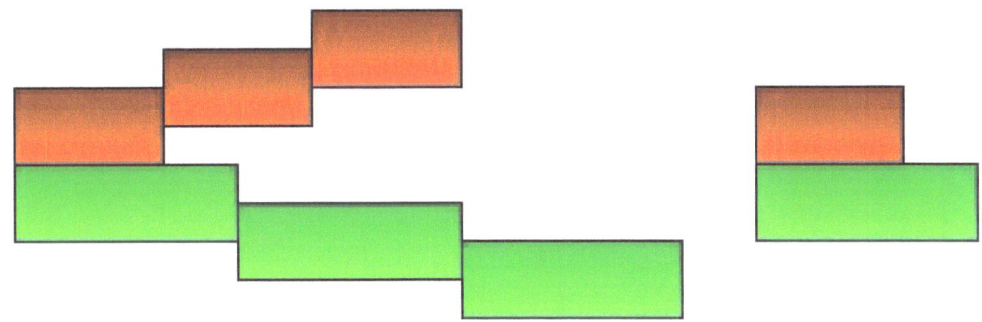

 Children have now found the first members of this particular family of equivalence, Adam and Eve – the irreducible pair.

 Try this with different pairs of trains as starting points.
Here are some examples with the irreducible pair in brackets:

(w, g)
(1, 3)
1/3

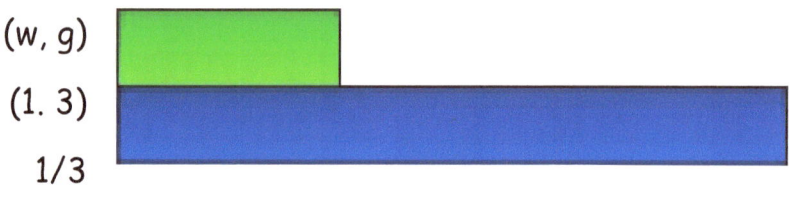

(g, p)
(3, 4)
3/4

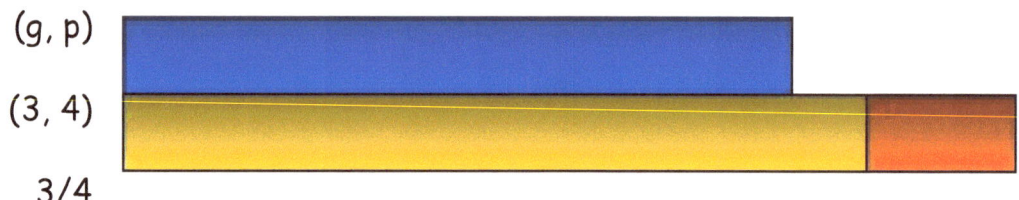

(r, y)
(2, 5)
2/5

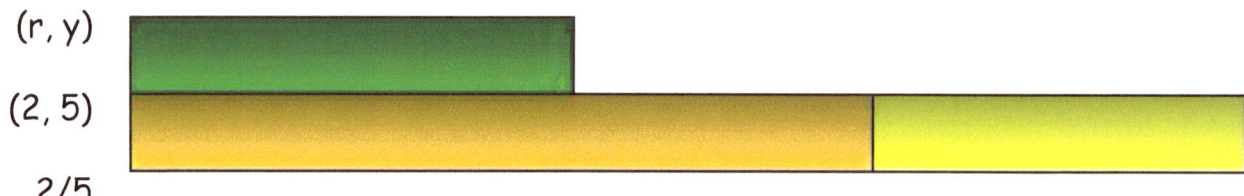

Example:
(w, g)
(1, 3)
1/3

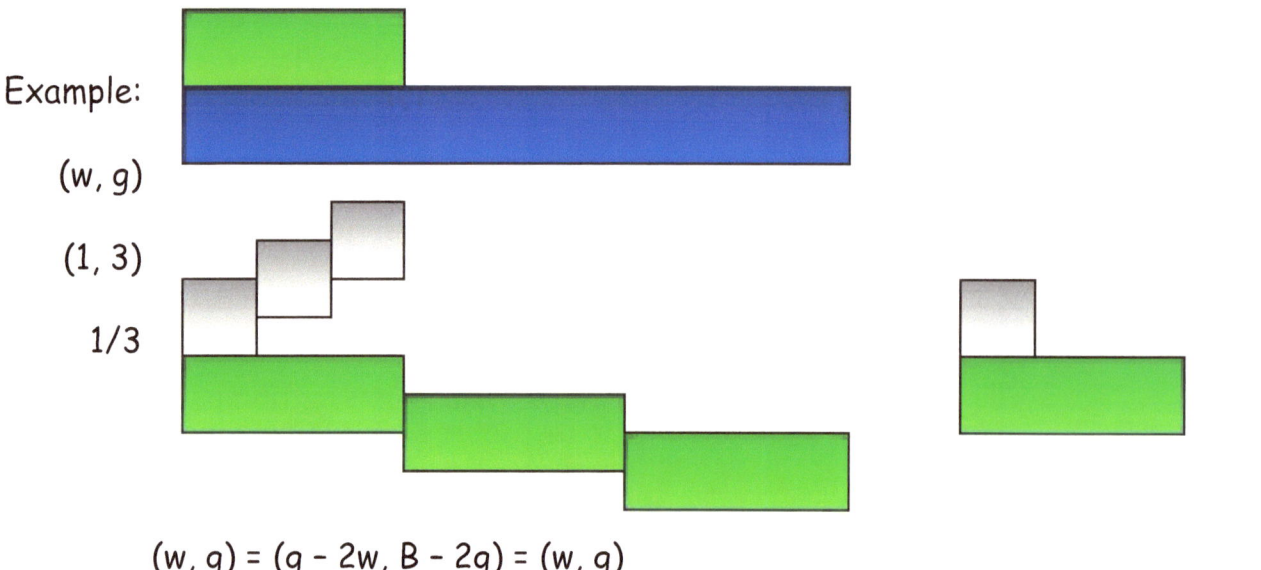

(w, g) = (g − 2w, B − 2g) = (w, g)

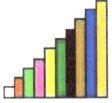 # UNIT 55: Families of Equivalent Fractions - Reproduction

FAMILIES OF EQUIVALENT FRACTIONS

Starting with the first pair of rods in the family– the irreducible pair – it is now possible to produce any other member of the family.

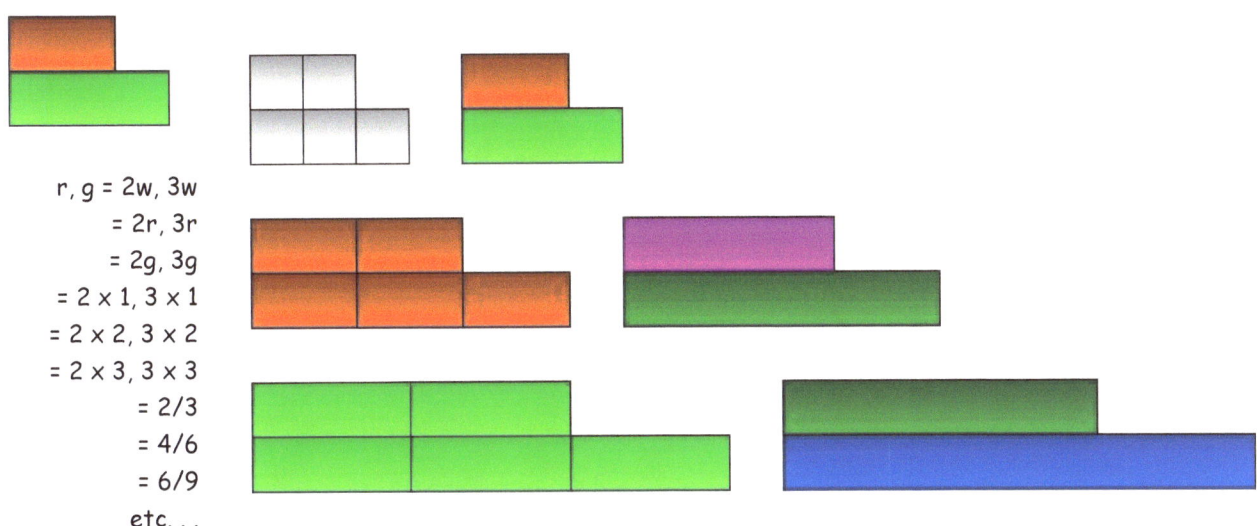

r, g = 2w, 3w
= 2r, 3r
= 2g, 3g
= 2 x 1, 3 x 1
= 2 x 2, 3 x 2
= 2 x 3, 3 x 3
= 2/3
= 4/6
= 6/9
etc...

Every pair can be reduced to white (1) – the lowest common denominator.

Or:

r, g = 2r, 2g
= 3r, 3g
= 2 x 2, 2 x 3
= 2 x 3, 3 x 3
= 2/3
= 4/6
= 6/9
etc...

Challenge children to find the sixth, seventh, eighth . . . member of the family.
Now try this with irreducible pairs such as:

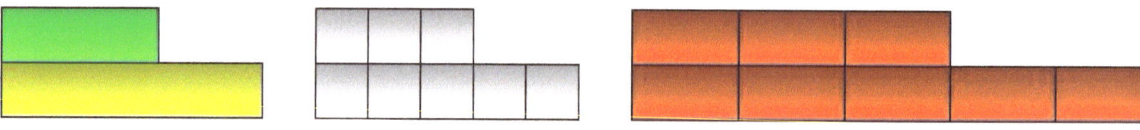

g, y = 3w, 5w = 3r, 5r = . . . 3, 5 = 3 x 1, 5 x 1 = 3 x 2, 5 x 2 =

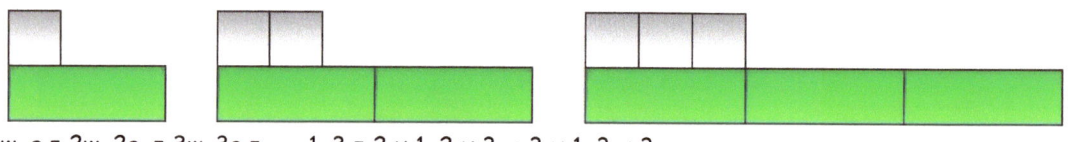

w, g = 2w, 2g, = 3w, 3g = . . . 1, 3 = 2 x 1, 2 x 3, = 3 x 1, 3 x 3

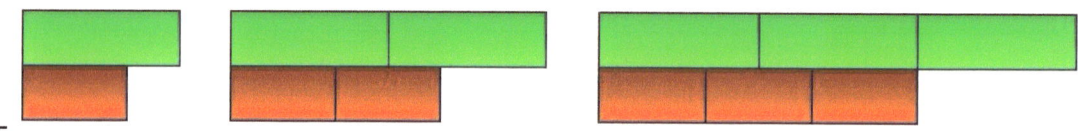

G, r = 2g, 2r = 3g, 3r = . . . 3, 2 = 2 x 3, 2 x 2 = 3 x 3, 3 x 2 =

Give plenty of examples of both approaches.

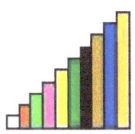 # UNIT 56: Families of Equivalent Addition

 FAMILIES OF EQUIVALENT ADDITION

Look at the trains below.

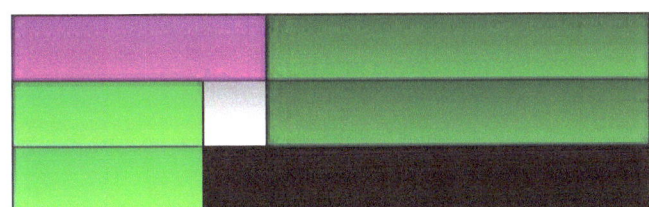

p + d = (g + w) + d = g +(w + d) = g + b

4 + 6 = (3 + 1) + 6 = 3 + (1 + 6) = 3 + 7

Instead of 'reading', "**pink plus dark green**", mentally substitute pink for two complementary rods (rods that together equal pink) such as: "**green plus white.**" Now read it again, this time saying "**white plus dark**" quickly to show you are grouping them together in brackets.

"What rods could you name instead of "white plus dark?"
"Can you substitute two rods for either green or black?"

For example: substituting green:

Read: "**Green plus black equals red plus . . . white and black. (say quickly)."**
"What rod could you name for white and black (tan)?"
3 + 7 = 2 + (1 + 7) = 2 + 8

Substituting black:

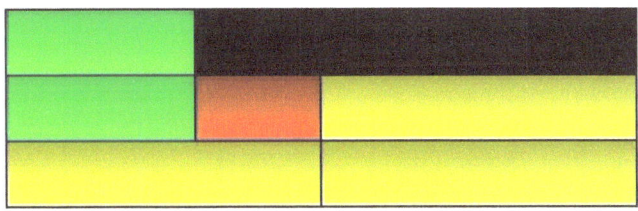

"**Green plus black equals green and red (say quickly). . . plus yellow.**"
"**What rod could you name for green and red (yellow)?**
3 + 7 = (3 + 2) + 5 = 5 + 5

Using this method help children to find all the other pairs equal to the first pair.

The table opposite is the complete table of colour/number pairs for orange/ten.

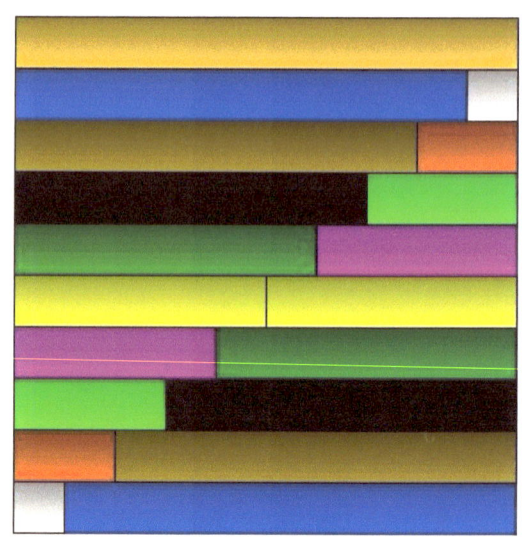

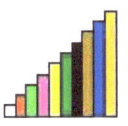 # UNIT 57: Families of Equivalent Products

 FAMILIES OF EQUIVALENT PRODUCTS

Three's A Crowd! - The associative and commutative properties of multiplication.

Using the commutative property is straightforward:

4d = 6p

4 x 6 = 6 x 4 = 24

Now the associative property is used:

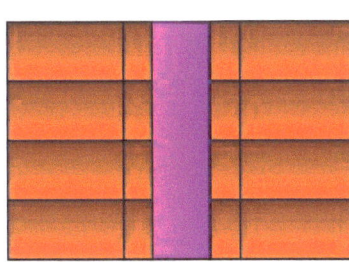

We can replace one dark green with three red rods:
3r x p =
(3 x 2) x 4 =

When we do this pink is left outside the brackets.

By putting brackets around the last two numbers we get:
g x (2p) =
3 x (2 x 4) =

This time green is left out in the cold!

For one rod (tan), we get::
g × t = t × g   3 × 8 = 8 × 3 (commutative)

 If we substitute 4 red rods for the tan we get:
g × (4r) =
3 × (4 × 2) =

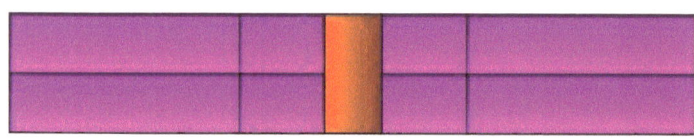 When we leave pink outside the bracket we get:
(3p) × r = (3 × 4) × 2 = (associative)

Because we do not have a rod equal to three pink rods we have to make a train:
12r = 2 × (o + r)
12 × 2 = 2 × 12

What we have found are members of the family of equivalent products of 24:
6 × 4 = 4 × 6 = 3 × 8 = 8 × 3 = 12 × 2 = 2 × 12 = . . .
. . . and we could have found more.

Ask children to find more equivalent relationships of:

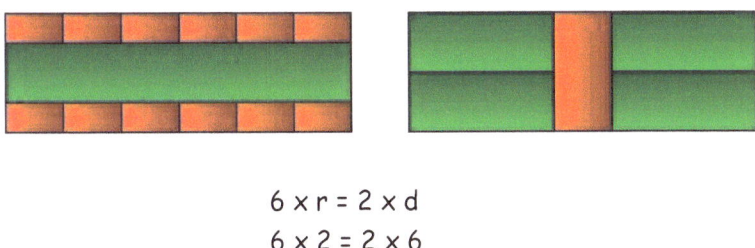

6 x r = 2 x d
6 x 2 = 2 x 6

Try this with different 'products'.
Extend the challenge by giving children just 'crosses' to start with:

Before we come to the end of this stage in children's mathematical development let us take one last look at fractions and see how we can move from one branch of the family to a completely different branch.

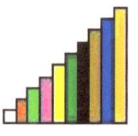 # UNIT 58: Families of Equivalent Fractions

 FAMILIES OF EQUIVALENT FRACTIONS

Moving from one family of equivalence to another.

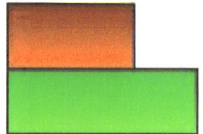      

The family of equivalence above reads:
r, g = p, d = d. B = 2/3 = 4/6 = 6/9 =

We saw how to find these family members in Units 46-48 and 52-55
But how do we get from one family of equivalence to another?

   Choose the first pair of rods, the irreducible pair, Adam and Eve.
Say:
"Add any rod you like to either the red or green rod."

He/she might choose, for example, yellow.
The choice would be to add the yellow to the top or bottom.

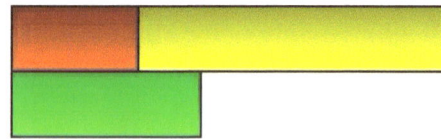

This would read: (r + y), g = 7/3 =

This would read: r, (g + y) = 2/8 =

We have moved easily from one family to another.

The challenge is now to find more members of the family.

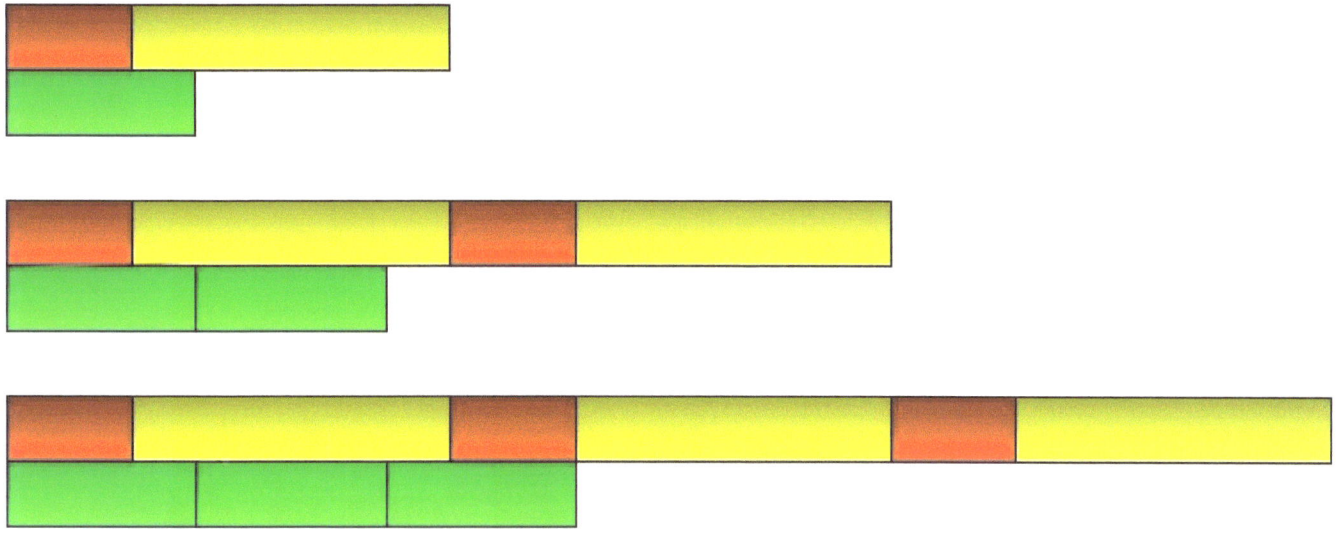

This would read:

(r + y), g = 2(r + y), 2g = 3(r + y), 3g = 7/3 = 14/6 = 21/9 =

Remind children of the games you played in Unit 52.

Now ask:

"Can you replace the rods with just one rod or a train, using the least number of rods possible (this usually makes children think of orange first, but not always)?"

They might produce this:

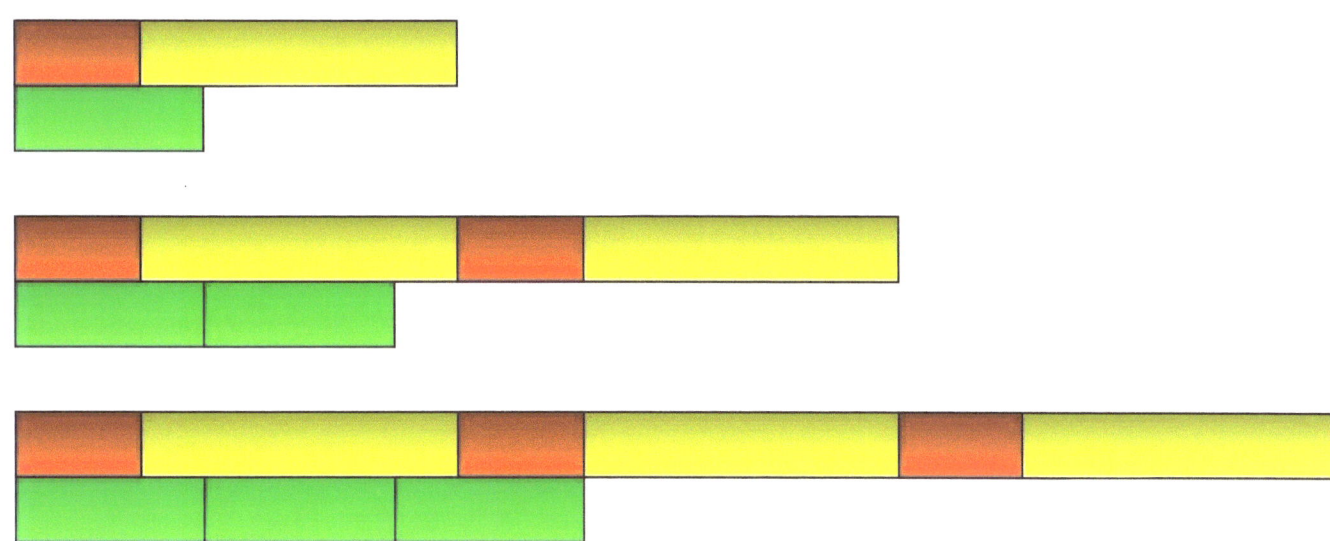

Remember **Cinderella's Staircase** (Unit 11)?
Staircases help us 'see' number sequences.

Say:
"Take the rods/trains on top and arrange them in a staircase. Do the same for the rods/trains on the bottom. Can you continue the staircase?"

In the first staircase each 'step' is equivalent to black rod.
In the second staircase each 'step' is equivalent to the green rod

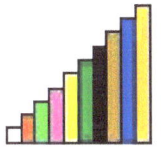# UNIT 59: Accelerated Learning

ACCELERATED LEARNING

Used imaginatively and creatively, as intended by their creator. Cuisenaire rods accelerate the learning process to a considerable degree.

Let us remind ourselves of some of the 'accelerated learning' processes they support:

 Enriched sensory stimulation.

The power of colour.

 Imagination better than knowledge.

Exploration and discovery- the rich landscape of pattern and relationships

 The 'Big Picture' - global overview.

Manual dexterity stimulates the brain.

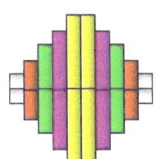 Imaging and memory recall.

Non-conscious, incidental learning.

 Discussion – the importance of talk.

'Reading trains' - the 'flow' state.

 Quality questions challenge the brain.

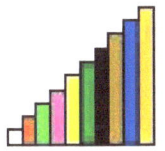

UNIT 60: Points Worth Remembering

 Always allow opportunity for free play it is the source of all future development.

 Ensure children have a clear mental image of the rods. Play plenty of 'touch' games.

 When introducing the signs give plenty of examples. e g **"What must I add to yellow, red, white, dark green to make a train equal to black?"**

 Spend time 'reading trains together as new signs are introduced.

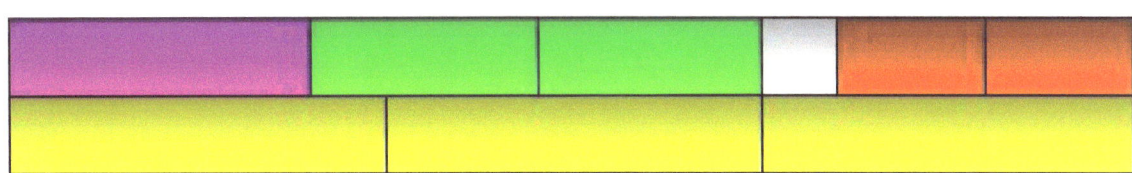

p + g + g + w + r + r = y + y + y   (Addition)
4 + 3 + 3 + 1 + 2 + 2 = 5 + 5 + 5

p + 2g + w + 2r = 3y (Multiplication and Addition)
4 + (2 x 3) + 1 + (2 x 2) = 3 x 5

$(y - w) + (b - p) + (p - w) + (g - r) + (p - r) + (y - g) =$
$(d - w) + (b - r) + (t - g)$ (Subtraction and Addition)
$(5 - 1) + (7 - 4) + (4 - 1) + (3 - 2) + (4 - 2) + (5 - 3) =$
$(6 - 1) + (7 - 2) + (8 - 3)$ (Using Compensatory Dynamics)

$(t \div 2) + (B \div 3) + (d \div 2) + (r \div 2) + (d \div 3) + (t \div 4) =$
$(o \div 2) + ((o + y) \div 3) + (2o \div 4)$ (Division and Addition)
$(8 \div 2) + (9 \div 3) + (6 \div 2) + (2 \div 2) + (6 \div 3) + (8 \div 4) = ($
$10 \div 2) + (15 \div 3) + (20 \div 4)$ (Using Compensatory Dynamics)

$(1/2 \times t) + (1/3 \times B) + (1/2 \times d) + (1/5 \times y) + (1/4 \times t) + (1/5 \times o) =$
$(1/2 \times o) + (1/4 \times 2o) + (1/6 \times 3o)$ (Fractions as Operators)
$(1/2 \times 8) + (1/3 \times 9) + (1/2 \times 6) + (1/5 \times 5) + (1/4 \times t) + (1/5 \times 10) =$
$(1/2 \times 10) + (1/4 \times 20) + (1/6 \times 30)$

There are obviously many more ways of 'reading' these trains as new signs are introduced.
The 'Name Game' (Unit) is designed to strengthen this ability and achieve the 'flow' state.

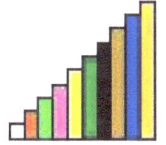

UNIT 61: Introducing Number Names

Your child has now been introduced to all the basic math concepts. He/she is able to 'read' a train in a variety of ways,

REMEMBER: The ability of children to use mental substitution is absolutely crucial when reading trains. After the rods have been put away ask questions to encourage mental visualization.

e g **"What two rods can I put end to end to equal yellow . . . etc.?**

At some point we shall introduce 'number names' for the rods. You are the best judge but I would suggest that number names are not adopted for the rods until the course has been completed.

Introducing 'number names'. It is vital that children do not think of a rod, say red, and a number, 2, as being one and the same.

Much of the time red will represent two but children must understand that it can also represent other numbers. Developing this kind of mental agility and the ability to abstract is crucial to children's mathematical development.

For example, when studying graphs this ability is fundamental.

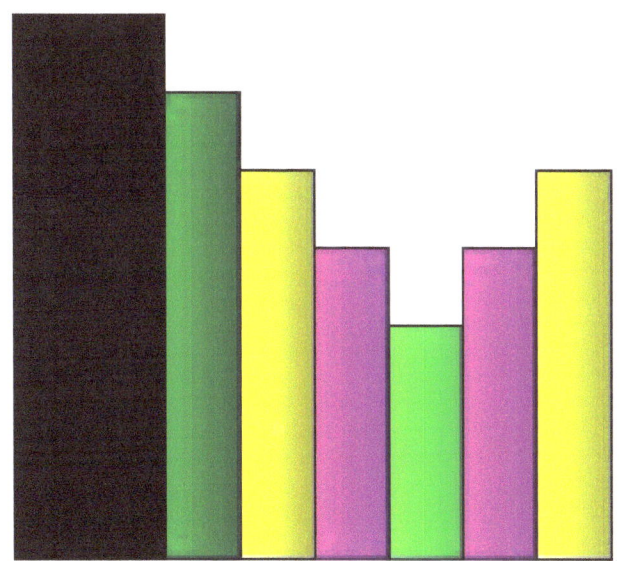

This block graph could be about anything from the fluctuating price of a stock price to my concentration span. They are both pretty similar.

Because children have already grasped the underlying concepts the transition from 'letter' to 'number' names will be completely painless.

Children have developed the ability to 'see' numbers as a whole (cardinal number) and not as a conglomeration of fragmented units aka 'counting on fingers'.

The prevailing climate throughout the course has been enjoyment through play, games and challenges in the form of questions.

The abiding principle is that children are **'learning how to learn'**.

How we introduce number is vital. Let us consider why.

The point is, if white represents one what is the value of pink or black? What if white were to represent 10 or 5? What would the value of black be now?

As in every family, everything is relative.

 # UNIT 62: Introducing Number Names Part 2

Life is all about relationships and so is maths. One family member behaves differently with different members of the same family. Relationships depend on the two members involved. This is also true, as we have seen, at the physical level. Mum can be taller than Billy but shorter than Dad.

For the most part white is going to represent 1, and so:

r = w + w   g = w + w + w   p = w + w + w + w
2 = 1 + 1   3 = 1 + 1 + 1   4 = 1 + 1 + 1 + 1

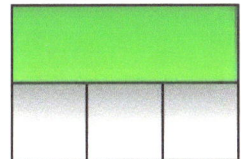

It is important to play games that 'change' the relationship.

 Say,
"If red represents 1 which rod represents 2, 3, 4 . . . ?"

Try this for other rods.

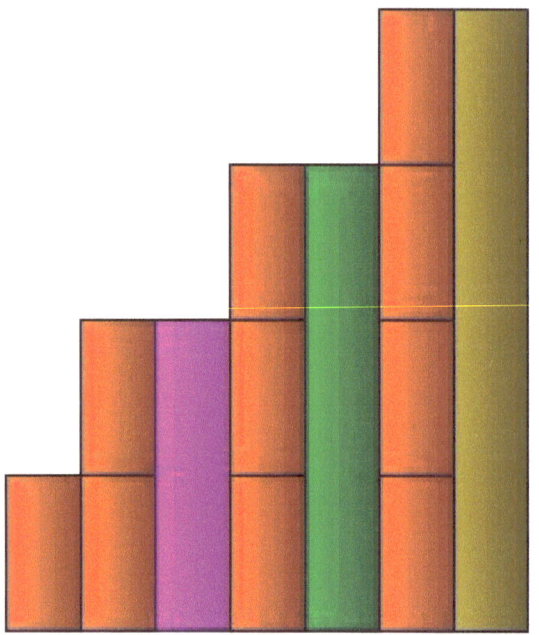 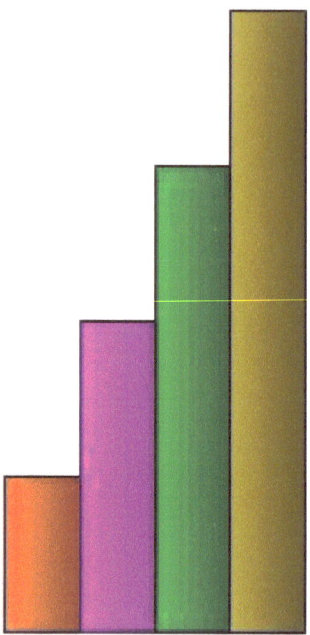

If red is 1, then pink is 2 because it is equivalent to 2 reds, dark green is 3 because it is equivalent to 3 reds, and so on.
Children may inquire about the white, green and yellow rod etc.

This is an opportunity to introduce the concept of fractions as numbers that exist between whole numbers

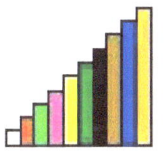# UNIT 63: Introducing Number Names Part 3

 EXTEND THE CHALLENGE.

Children will already have studied fractions as operators.
He/she will also have played the 'name game' - the concept that numbers, like people, can have more than one name depending on family relationships.
Now increase the challenge.

"If blue represents 1, what is the value of green?"

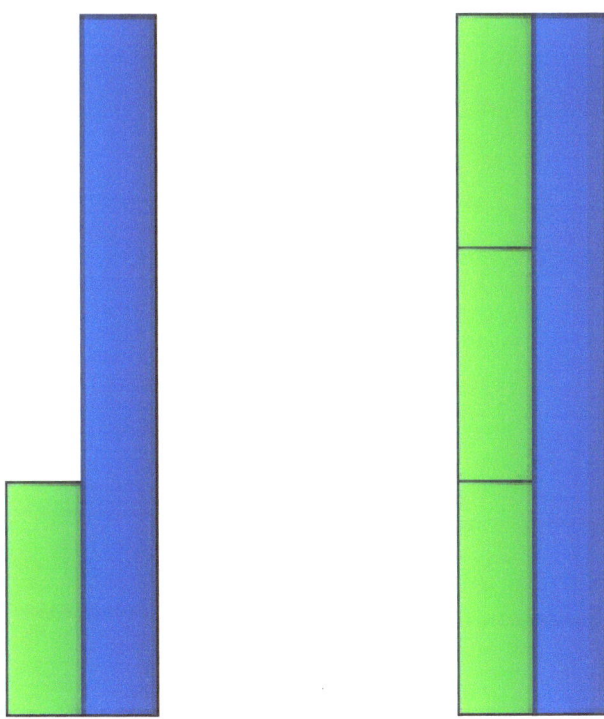

Say,

"How many green rods are equal to the blue rod?

So how many times bigger than the green is the blue rod?

How many times smaller than the blue rod is the green rod?

Do you remember the name we gave to say something was three times smaller? (One third)

Green is a third of blue.
Three is a third of nine."

Once you have introduced the concept of number it is a good idea to begin every shared session with the rods with a game of this type.

"if orange is 1, what is the value of yellow, white, red . . . ?

"If tan is 1, what is the value of red, white, pink . . . ?

By now you will be able to think of many examples for yourself.

UNIT 64: Journey's End?

JOURNEY'S END?

That's a question only you can answer.
I hope you have enjoyed the journey together with your children.
There is much left to explore but now you children should be equipped to do so in confidence.

The next book will focus on the structure of number and shall remain true to the philosophy of not imposing ready-made solutions upon children.
The guiding principle will always be exploration and self-discovery.
The only learning that is truly worth while.

Children will be introduced to a variety of number systems (bases of numeration) via the rods. They will explore these systems before being introduced to the decimal system which convention dictates we use universally.

This leads to the more formal structure of maths. However the freedom children have experienced throughout the program will empower them to think 'outside the box'.

Conventional approaches will not be a problem. They will also possess the mental agility to employ their own strategies using concepts like compensatory dynamics.

There is no danger of them being led blindfold down well worn paths dependent on the step by step guidance of any one individual.

Thanks and Bon Voyage!
Phil Rowlands
www.helpyourchildsucceed.com

Software Link - Please Copy and Paste.

http://www.helpyourchildsucceed.com/softwareapp.htm

You may also be interested in. . .

The Amazing Colour Factor Number Square

This program builds on '**Child's Play Maths 1 & 2**'.

The **Colour Square** is a physical resource that can be photocopied or removed from the back page of the book. It supports children's development in the following key areas:

- multiplication - products and factors, sequence of 'tables', the commutative property;
- square numbers
- division - with and without remainders;
- fractions as operators;
- factors - 'factors tables';
- prime numbers;
- graphs and averages;
- Pythagoras Theorem.

The **Colour Square** can be printed, photocopied and laminated as many times as necessary to provide every child with their own copy.
Please only distribute within your own group or school. **The Amazing Colour Factor Number Square** is now available on Amazon.

www.ingramcontent.com/pod-product-compliance
Lightning Source LLC
Chambersburg PA
CBHW041510220426
43661CB00047B/1526